Since their return to the galaxy, the Wulfen have been hunted down and found by members of the Space Wolves Chapter. Returned to the Fang on Fenris, they have been re-equipped ready for war.

Depuis leur retour dans la galaxie, les Wulfen ont été cherchés et retrouvés par leurs frères du chapitre des Space Wolves. Ramenés au Croc sur Fenris, ils ont été rééquipés et apprêtés pour la guerre.

Seit ihrer Rückkehr in die Galaxis wurden die Wulfen vom Orden der Space Wolves gejagt und aufgespürt. Nachdem sie zum Reißzahn auf Fenris zurückgebracht wurden, wurden sie neu ausgestattet.

The Wulfen wear modified power armour constructed to fit their altered physiology. You can also clearly see the infamous Black Carapace of the Space Marines, into which power armour plugs.

Les Wulfen portent des armures modifiées pour épouser leur physique altéré. En outre, vous pouvez voir sur eux la Carapace Noire des Space Marines, sur laquelle se connectent leurs armures énergétiques.

Wulfen tragen an ihre veränderte Physiologie angepasste Servorüstung. Du kannst deutlich den berühmten Schwarzen Panzer der Space Marines sehen, mit dem Servorüstungen verbunden werden.

The Wulfen leap into battle alongside their Chapter brethren. Too feral to use guns, many wear stormfrag auto-launchers on their backpacks that fire out a hail of high-explosive grenades as they advance.

Les Wulfen bondissent au combat aux côtés de leurs frères de chapitre. Trop sauvages pour utiliser des armes de tir, beaucoup ont sur le dos un auto-lanceur Stormfrag qui tire des grenades tandis qu'ils avancent.

Die Wulfen springen neben ihren Ordensbrüdern in die Schlacht. Da sie zu wild für Schusswaffen sind, tragen viele Sturmsplitter-Salvengranatwerfer, die hochexplosive Granaten regnen lassen.

IRON PRIEST

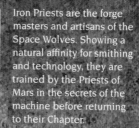

Iron Priests are the forge masters and artisans of the Space Wolves. Showing a natural affinity for smithing and technology, they are trained by the Priests of Mars in the secrets of the machine before returning to their Chapter.

Les Iron Priests sont les maîtres de forge et artisans des Space Wolves. Ayant une affinité naturelle avec la technologie, ils sont initiés par les Prêtres de Mars aux secrets de la machine avant de retourner au sein de leur chapitre.

Iron Priests sind die Schmiedemeister und Handwerker der Space Wolves. Wegen ihrer Affinität für das Schmieden und Technologie wurden sie von den Priestern des Mars in den Geheimnissen der Maschine unterwiesen.

The Iron Priest carries a thunder hammer and a helfrost pistol, both likely to have been crafted by his own hand. A heavy-duty servo-arm is mounted on his backpack, its jaws cast in the shape of a Fenrisian wolf's head.

L'Iron Priest porte un marteau Thunder et un pistolet Helfrost, tous deux fabriqués de ses propres mains. Un servo-bras est monté sur son paquetage, ses mâchoires forgées à l'effigie d'une tête de loup de Fenris.

Der Iron Priest trägt einen Energiehammer und eine Helfrost-Pistole, die er wahrscheinlich selbst geschmiedet hat. Ein Servoarm sitzt am Rückenmodul, seine Kiefer Haben die Form eines fenrisischen Wolfskopfs.

The Iron Priest wears an ancient suit of runic armour, its panels covered in pipes, crenellations, cables and wolf pelts. It also incorporates a bionic arm, the sign of a once-grievous injury.

L'Iron Priest porte une ancienne armure dont les plaques sont couvertes de câbles, de créneaux et de peau de loup. Il arbore également un bras bionique, signe d'une grave blessure reçue jadis.

Der Iron Priest trägt eine uralte Runenrüstung, die von Röhren, Zinnenmustern, Kabeln und Wolfspelz bedeckt ist. Sie hat auch einen bionischen Arm als Zeichen einer ehemals schweren Verwundung.

ULRIK THE SLAYER

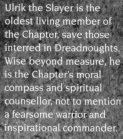

Ulrik the Slayer is the oldest living member of the Chapter, save those interred in Dreadnoughts. Wise beyond measure, he is the Chapter's moral compass and spiritual counsellor, not to mention a fearsome warrior and inspirational commander.

Dreadnoughts mis à part, Ulrik the Slayer est le doyen des Space WOlves. Sage sans commune mesure, il est le sens moral du chapitre et un grand conseiller spirituel, sans oublier un redoutable guerrier et un officier au charisme exceptionnel.

Ulrik the Slayer ist das älteste lebende Ordens-mitglied, abgesehen jener in Dreadnoughts. Er ist weise und der moralische Kompass und geistige Ratgeber des Ordens, dazu ein furchterregender Krieger und inspirierender Befehlshaber.

As the Chapter's Wolf High Priest, Ulrik wears the Wolf Helm of Russ, a relic said to have been given to Russ by the Emperor himself. Stoic, calm and calculating, Ulrik is seen here surveying the battlefield before him, his crozius arcanum held ready at his side.

En tant que Haut Prêtre Loup, Ulrik porte le Heaume du Loup de Russ, une relique dont on raconte qu'elle fut offerte à Russ par l'Empereur en personne. Stoïque et calculateur, Ulrik surveille le champ de bataille devant lui, son crozius arcanum à son côté.

Als Hoher Wolf Priest trägt Ulrik den Wolfshelm des Russ, eine Reliquie, die Russ vom Imperator selbst erhalten haben soll. Stoisch, ruhig und berechnend überlickt Ulrik hier das Schlachtfeld vor sich und hält sein Crozius Arcanum bereit.

Ulrik the Slayer surveys the battlefield as Harald Deathwolf's Great Company march to war supported by the newly-found Wulfen.

Ulrik the Slayer observe le champ de bataille pendant que la Grande Compagnie de Harald Deathwolf avance, appuyée par les Wulfen.

Ulrik the Slayer überblickt das Schlachtfeld, als Harald Deathwolfs Great Company unterstützt von den Wulfen in den Krieg zieht.

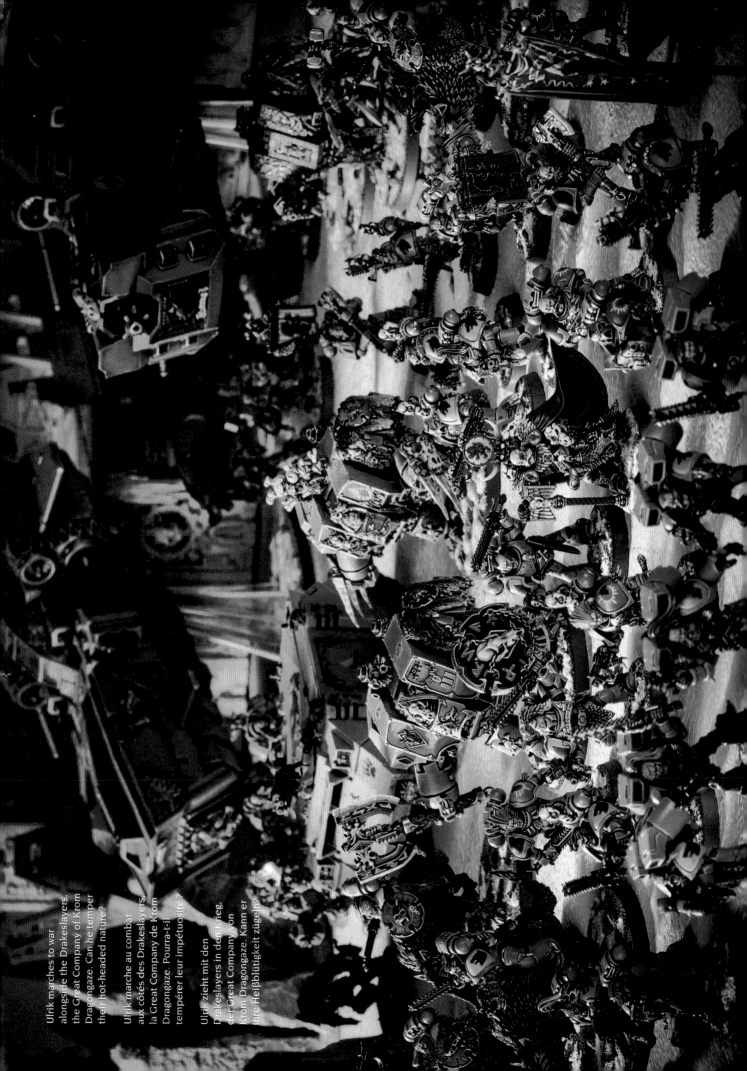

Ulrik marches to war alongside the Drakeslayers, the Great Company of Krom Dragongaze. Can he temper their hot-headed nature?

Ulrik marche au combat aux côtés des Drakeslayers, la Great Company de Krom Dragongaze. Pourra-t-il tempérer leur impétuosité ?

Ulrik zieht mit den Drakeslayers in den Krieg, der Great Company von Krom Dragongaze. Kann er ihre Heißblütigkeit zügeln?

Ulrik the Slayer earned his title during the First War for Armageddon. He killed three Khorne Berzerkers with his bare hands, earning a grim salute from Angron himself.

Ulrik the Slayer gagna son titre durant la Première Guerre d'Armageddon. Il tua trois Khorne Berzerkers à main nue, ce qui lui vallut le salut d'Angron en personne.

Ulrik the Slayer verdiente seinen Titel im Ersten Krieg um Armageddon. Er rötete drei Khorne-Berserker mit bloßen Händen, wofür Angron ihm salutierte.

THE WULFEN RETURNED

On worlds all across the galaxy the Wulfkind have returned, the 13th Company of the Space Wolves Chapter. Seen as an omen, it is said their reappearance will herald the return of Leman Russ, the Primarch of the Space Wolves. Whether this will come to pass remains to be seen, though one clear fact remains – should others witness the Wulfen, questions will be asked about the purity of the Space Wolves' bloodline. And so, for the first time in thousands of years, the Space Wolves Chapter in its entirety heads for the stars in search of its lost brothers. But what fate awaits the brave Sons of Russ and their long-lost kin?

Les Wulfkin, 13ᵉ Cⁱᵉ des Space Wolves, ont réapparu sur plusieurs mondes à travers la galaxie. Tel un présage, on raconte que leur retour annonce celui de Leman Russ, le Primarch des Space Wolves. Que cela s'avère reste encore à voir, mais un fait demeure certain : si les Wulfen sont vus par d'autres instances impériales, la pureté de la lignée des fils de Russ pourrait être remise en question. Ainsi, pour la première fois de puis des millénaires, les Space Wolves au grand complet s'élancent à travers la mer d'étoiles à la recherche de leurs frères perdus. Mais quel sort attend les braves fils de Russ et leur parenté depuis longtemps égarée ?

Auf Welten überall in der Galaxis kehren die Wulfen zurück, die 13. Company des Ordens der Space Wolves. Für Manchen ist dies ein Omen, das der Rückkehr von Leman Russ vorausgeht, dem Primarch der Space Wolves. Ob dies der Wahrheit entspricht, wird sich zeigen, doch eines ist offensichtlich: Wenn andere der Wulfen ansichtig werden, werden Fragen bezüglich der Reinheit der Blutlinie der Space Wolves aufkommen. Und so zieht zum ersten Mal seit Jahrtausenden der ganze Orden der Space Wolves aus, um die verlorenen Brüder zu suchen. Welches Schicksal mag die tapferen Söhne des Russ und ihre endlich zurückkehrenden Brüder erwarten?

The warriors of Harald Deathwolf's Great Company, accompanied by Logan Grimnar himself, smash into the Tyranids of Hive Fleet Leviathan.

Les guerriers de la Great Company de Harald Deathwolf, accompagnés par Logan Grimnar, ravagent les tyranids de la flotte-ruche Leviathan.

Die Krieger von Harald Deathwolfs Great Company, begleitet von Logan Grimnar selbst, greifen die Tyraniden von Schwarmflotte Leviathan an.

Even the near-death experience of being interred in a Dreadnought was not enough to stave off the Curse of the Wulfen for the unfortunate Murderfang.

Même frôler la mort et être incarcéré dans un Dreadnought ne suffit pas à empêcher la malédiction du Wulfen de frapper l'infortuné Murderfang.

Selbst die Nahtodeserfahrung, in einem Dreadnought beigesetzt zu sein, reichte nicht, den Fluch des Wulfen vom armen Murderfang fernzuhalten.

WOLF LORD KROM

Krom Dragongaze is Wolf Lord of the Drakeslayers, a ferocious warrior who revels in the thrill of battle and the spilling of his enemies' blood. Known as Fierce-eye by his peers, he can see a foe's weakness before they even know they have one.

Krom Dragongaze est le Wolf Lord des Drakeslayers, un guerrier féroce qui se délecte du frisson du combat et de verser le sang de l'adversaire. Appelé Œil Féroce par ses pairs, il peut déceler les faiblesses de ses ennemis avant même qu'ils en aient conscience.

Krom Dragongaze ist Wolf Lord der Drakeslayers, ein wilder Krieger, der den Nervenkitzel der Schlacht und das Blutvergießen genießt. Seine Brüder kennen ihn als Wildauge und er erkennt Schwächen der Feinde, ehe sie wissen, dass sie eine haben.

Krom's armour is decorated with Fenrisian runes, the Belt of Russ worn around his waist a symbol of his rank. In one hand he wields a bolt pistol, its targeter linked to his bionic eye. In the other he carries Wyrmclaw, a well-balanced and finely-crafted frost axe.

L'armure de Krom est ornée de runes de Fenris, et la Ceinture de Russ à sa taille est un symbole de son rang. D'une main, il tient un pistolet bolter au viseur relié à son œil bionique. De l'autre il brandit Wyrmclaw, sa hache de givre ciselée et parfaitement équilibrée.

Kroms Rüstung ist mit fenrisischen Runen dekoriert, der Gürtel des Russ um seine Hüften zeigt seinen Rang. In einer Hand hält er eine Boltpistole, die mit seinem bionischen Auge verbunden ist, in der anderen Wyrmklaue, eine gut balancierte Frostaxt.

Krom leads his Wolf Guard into battle against the Orks on the world of Alaric Prime. It proved to be a painful defeat for the proud son of Russ.

Krom mène ses Wolf Guard au combat face aux orks sur le monde d'Alaric Prime. Cela s'avéra une cuisante défaite pour les fiers fils de Russ.

Krom führt seine Wolf Guard auf Alaric Primus gegen die Orks. Es sollte eine schmerzhafte Niederlage für die Söhne des Russ werden.

TAU EMPIRE

COALITION COMMAND

Tau Hunter Cadres are often led by a Fire caste Commander and an Ethereal, the former planning the army's method of attack, the latter keeping a watchful eye on the well-being of its soldiers.

Les Tau Hunter Cadres sont souvent dirigés par un Commander de la caste du Feu et un Ethereal, le premier planifiant les attaques, le second gardant un œil attentif sur le bien-être de ses soldats.

Hunter Cadres werden oft von Commanders der Feuerkaste und einem Ethereal geführt, wobei Ersterer die Angriffsweise der Armee plant und Letzterer ein wachsames Auge auf das Wohl der Soldaten hat.

Tau Commanders wear the most advanced battlesuits in the Earth caste armoury. Their latest innovation is the XV86 Coldstar Battlesuit (shown above) that enables the pilot to fly across the battlefield.

Les Tau Commanders porte les axo-armures les plus avancées de l'arsenal de la caste de la Terre. Leur dernière inovation est la XV86 Coldstar Battlesuit (ci)dessus) qui peut voler à travers le champ de bataille.

Commanders der Tau haben die besten Battlesuits des Arsenals der Erdkaste. Ihre neuste Erfindung ist der XV86 Coldstar Battlesuit (siehe oben), mit dem der Pilot über das Schlachtfeld fliegen kann.

Tau Ethereals are mysterious beings, maintaining a spiritual hold over their fellow Tau, encouraging them to great acts of bravery and fortitude. This Ethereal floats imperiously into battle on a Hover Drone.

Les Tau Ethereals sont des êtres mystérieux qui maintiennent une emprise spirituelle sur les autres Tau, les poussant à des actes de bravoure. Cet Ethereal flotte impérieusement sur un Hover Drone.

Ethereals sind geheimnis-volle Wesen, die ein spirituelles Band zu anderen Tau haben, durch das sie sie zu Mut und Stär-ke inspirieren. Dieser Ethe-real schwebt gebieterisch auf einer Hover Drone in die Schlacht.

With the tactical guidance of a Battlesuit Commander and the inspiring presence of an Ethereal, the Fire Warriors of Vior'la advance upon the foe.

Avec la maîtrise tactique d'un Commander en exo-armure et la présence galvanisante d'un Ethereal, les Fire Warriors de Vior'la avancent vers l'ennemi.

Mit der taktischen Führung eines Battlesuit Commanders und der Präsenz eines Ethereals im Rücken rücken die Fire Warriors von Vior'la gegen den Feind vor.

Commanders who pilot the XV86 Coldstar Battlesuit are invariably hot-headed warriors. They often lead from the front, striking at the heart of the enemy army.

Les Commanders qui pilotent une XV86 Coldstar Battlesuit sont invariablement impétueux. Souvent en première ligne, ils frappent au cœur de l'armée adverse.

Commanders in einem XV86 Coldstar Battlesuit sind ausnahmslos hitzköpfige Krieger. Sie führen von vorn und schlagen mitten in das Herz des Feindes.

The might of Vior'la descends on the Blood Angels. At the head of the assault, Ethereal Aun'Ko faces the enemies of the Greater Good with steely determination.

La puissance de Vior'la s'abat sur les Blood Angels. À la tête de l'assaut, l'Ethereal Aun'Ko affronte les ennemis du Bien Suprême avec détermination.

Die Macht von Vior'la fällt über die Blood Angels her. An der Spitze des Angriffs stellt sich Ethereal Aun'Ko eisern gegen die Feinde des Höheren Wohls.

WARBOSS GRUKK'S BOSS-MOB

Grukk Face-rippa is the Warboss responsible for the Red Waaagh! terrorising the area of Imperial space known as Sanctus Reach. Though presumed dead, Grukk has a nasty habit of reappearing where the fighting is thickest.

Grukk Face-rippa est le Warboss responsable de la Red Waaagh! terrorisant la zone impériale appelée Sanctus Reach. Présumé mort, Grukk a la sale habitude de réapparaître où les combats sont les plus âpres.

Der Warboss Grukk Face-rippa ist für den Roten Waaagh verantwortlich, der die Sanctus Reach plagt. Er wird für tot gehalten, doch taucht lästigerweise immer wieder da auf, wo am härtesten gekämpft wird.

Grukk earned his grizzly moniker after brutally defacing his former Warboss using his own power claw. Grukk subsequently claimed the weapon for his own, its revving buzz-saw a constant worry to nearby greenskins.

Grukk gagna son surnom macabre après avoir défiguré son précédent Warboss avec sa propre pince énergétique. Grukk récupéra l'arme, dont la scie circulaire rugissante constitue une constante menace pour les peaux-vertes à proximité.

Grukk erhielt seinen brutalen Beinamen nachdem er seinem vorherigen Warboss mit dessen Energieklauä das Gesicht abriss. Er nahm die Waffe an sich und ihr Klang ist allen Grünhäuten in der Nähe eine Warnung

Grukk is accompanied by his Boss-Mob, a group of the hardest, most killy Orks around. They know that wherever Grukk is, that's where the best fight will be.

Grukk est accompagné de sa Boss-Mob, un groupe composé ses orks les plus meurtriers du coin. Ils savent qu'où que se rende Grukk, les combats seront les meilleurs.

Grukk begleitet sein Boss-Mob, eine Gruppe der härtesten, tödlichsten Orks. Sie wissen, dass da, wo Grukk ist, auch der beste Kampf ist.

The Red Waaagh! also includes a large contingent of Bad Moons led by the vicious Big Mek Mogrok. It's rumoured that Mogrok engineered Grukk's death.

La Red Waaagh! comprend également un vaste contingent de Bad Moons menés par le Big Mek Mogrok. Selon la rumeur, c'est lui qui aurait arrangé la mort de Grukk.

Der Rote Waaagh enthält ein großes Kontingent Bad Moons unter dem Kommando von Big Mek Mogrok. Es heißt, er habe Grukks Tod herbeigeführt.

Grukk's greatest battle was against the Space Wolves of Krom Dragongaze's Great Company, a fight that saw both commanders bloodied and humiliated.

Grukk livra son plus beau combat contre les Space Wolves de la Great Company de Krom Dragongaze, une lutte qui laissa les deux commandants ensanglantés et humiliés.

Grukks größte Schlacht war gegen die Great Company von Krom Dragongaze, ein Kampf, in dem beide Befehlshaber Blut ließen und Demütigung erfuhren.

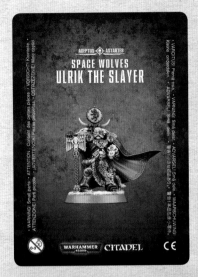

ADEPTUS ASTARTES
SPACE WOLVES ULRIK THE SLAYER
WARHAMMER 40,000 · CITADEL

ADEPTUS ASTARTES
SPACE WOLVES WULFEN
5 MINIATURES
WARHAMMER 40,000

ADEPTUS ASTARTES
SPACE WOLVES IRON PRIEST
WARHAMMER 40,000 · CITADEL

TAU EMPIRE
COALITION COMMAND
3 MINIATURES
WARHAMMER 40,000

ADEPTUS ASTARTES
SPACE WOLVES WOLF LORD KROM
WARHAMMER 40,000 · CITADEL

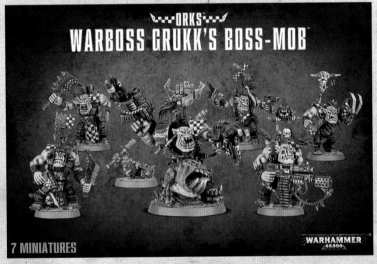

ORKS
WARBOSS GRUKK'S BOSS-MOB
7 MINIATURES
WARHAMMER 40,000

LATEST RELEASES

SPACE WOLVES WULFEN
5 miniatures – the 13th Company return!

£35, €45, 350dkr, 420skr, 390nkr, 175zł, USA $60, Can $70,
AU $100, NZ $115, ¥8,000, 350rmb, HK$475, R215, SG$85

SPACE WOLVES IRON PRIEST
1 miniature – the warrior-smiths of Space Wolves!

£18.50, €25, 190dkr, 220skr, 200nkr, 93zł, USA $30, Can $35,
AU $50, NZ $60, ¥4,500, 190rmb, HK$250, R115, SG$45

SPACE WOLVES ULRIK THE SLAYER
1 miniature – chief amongst the Wolf Priests, one of the Space Wolves' mightiest heroes!

£18.50, €25, 190dkr, 220skr, 200nkr, 93zł, USA $30, Can $35,
AU $50, NZ $60, ¥4,500, 190rmb, HK$250, R115, SG$45

SPACE WOLVES WOLF LORD KROM
1 miniature – Krom Dragongaze, Wolf Lord of the Drakeslayers Great Company.

£18.50, €25, 190dkr, 220skr, 200nkr, 93zł, USA $30, Can $35,
AU $50, NZ $60, ¥4,500, 190rmb, HK$250, R115, SG$45

WARBOSS GRUKK'S BOSS-MOB
7 miniatures – Grukk Face-rippa and some equally face-ripping Ork Nobs.

£32.50, €45, 340dkr, 400skr, 385nkr, 160zł, USA $50, Can $65,
AU $90, NZ $105, ¥7,500, 320rmb, HK$435, R200, SG$75

TAU EMPIRE COALITION COMMAND
3 miniatures – A Tau Battlesuit Commander and Ethereal to lead your cadre.

£37.50, €50, 375dkr, 450skr, 415nkr, 190zł, USA $60, Can $75,
AU $105, NZ $125, ¥8,700, 375rmb, HK$510, R230, SG$90

ARMY OF THE MONTH

Storming into Army of the Month this month is a massive army of Red Scorpions painted by Ben Ballard, a collection he's been working on for the last three years. Turn the page to see more of his impressive strike force.

Army of the Month est pris d'assaut ce mois-ci par une énorme armée de Red Scorpions peinte par Ben Ballard, une collection sur laquelle il a consacré les trois dernières années. Tournez la page pour découvrir cette force monumentale.

Diesen Monat stürmt eine gewaltige Army of the Month der Red Scorpions, bemalt von Ben Ballard, diesen Artikel. An dieser Sammlung arbeitet er seit drei Jahren. Blättere um und sieh mehr von dieser beeindruckenden Streitmacht.

"I've been collecting since the days of Rogue Trader," says Ben. "I reckon I've collected something of everything over the years, but the Red Scorpions are definitely my largest project to date."

"Je collectionne depuis l'époque de Rogue Trader," confie Ben. "J'avoue avoir collectionné à peu près de tout au fil des ans, mais les Red Scorpions sont sans conteste mon projet le plus vaste jusqu'à présent."

„Ich sammle schon seit Rogue-Trader-Zeiten", sagt Ben. „Ich denke, ich habe im Lauf der Jahre schon von allem etwas gesammelt, aber die Red Scorpions sind definitiv mein größtes Projekt bisher."

"I was inspired to paint my Space Marines as Red Scorpions after seeing them in the Anphelion Project book by Forge World. They've got a rich and exciting background with loads of great artwork."

"J'ai voulu peindre mes Space Marines en Red Scorpions après les avoir admirés dans le livre Anphelion Project de Forge World. Ils ont une histoire riche et palpitante accompagnée de superbes illustrations."

„Ich wurde vom Anphelion-Project-Buch von Forge World inspiriert, meine Space Marines als Red Scorpions zu bemalen. Sie haben einen reichen und aufregenden Hintergrund und tolles Artwork."

Ben's collection includes miniatures from the last few decades, some metal, some resin, some plastic. The Chaplain on the right is even made of lead!

La collection de Ben inclut des figurines des dernières décennies, certaines en métal, d'autres en résine ou en plastique. Le Chaplain de droite est même en plomb !

Bens Sammlung enthält Modelle aus ein paar Dekaden, manche Metall, manche Resin, manche Kunststoff. Der Chaplain rechts ist sogar noch aus Blei gegossen!

All the models in Ben's army were based using chunks of slate and tufts of dry grass from the Warhammer 40,000 basing kit (well, quite a few kits, actually).

Toutes les figurines de l'armée de Ben ont été soclées avec de l'ardoise et des touffes d'herbe du kit de soclage Warhammer 40,000 (en fait, d'un certain nombre de ces kits).

Alle Modelle erhielten eine Basegestaltung aus Schiefer und trockenem Gras aus dem Warhammer-40.000-Basegestaltungsset (einer Menge Sets tatsächlich).

There are three Command Squads in Ben's army, this one featuring both Citadel and Forge World models. Ben used blue object source lighting on all the power weapons, lights and lascannons in the army.

L'armée de Ben compte 3 Command Squads, celle-ci comprenant des figurines Citadel et Forge World. Ben a utilisé un effet de lumière directionnel bleuté sur tous les canons laser, lumières et armes énergétiques de l'armée.

Bens Armee enthält drei Command Squads, dieses enthält Modelle von Forge World und Citadel. Ben malte blaue gerichtete Lichteffekte auf Energiewaffen, Lichter und Laserkanonen der Armee.

With so many vehicles in his army, it seemed only right for Ben to include a contingent of Techmarines. Ben also converted his Thunderfire Cannon (below) to look like it's firing.

Avec tant de véhicules dans son armée, il semblait logique pour Ben d'inclure un contingent de Techmarines. Ben a également converti son Thunderfire Cannon (ci-dessous) pour donner l'impression qu'il tire.

Bei so vielen Fahrzeugen in der Armee schien es nur richtig, ein Kontingent Techmarines mitzunehmen. Ben baute auch die Thunderfire Cannon (unten) so um, dass sie aussieht, als ob sie feuert..

Conclave includes three generations of Librarian miniatures representing many years of collecting.

Conclave de Ben comprend trois générations de figurines, qui représentent de nombreuses années à collectionner.

Librarius Conclave drei Generationen von Librarian-Miniaturen, die lange Jahre des Sammelns repräsentieren..

Magister Sevrin Loth (below on the left) is the Chief Librarian of the Red Scorpions. Ben used the Honour Guard that comes with him as his Commander's bodyguards.

Sevrin Loth (ci-dessous à gauche) est le Chief Librarian des Red Scorpions. Ben a utilisé les Honour Guard fournis avec lui comme gardes du corps de son commander.

Magister Sevrin Loth (unten links) ist der Chief Librarian der Red Scorpions. Ben teilte Loths Honour Guards seinem Commander als Leibwache zu.

Opposite: Every unit in the strike force has a dedicated transport, be it a Rhino, a Land Raider or, in the case of these Tactical Squads, a Drop Pod.

Ci-contre : chaque unité de la force de frappe possède un transport assigné, qu'il s'agisse d'un Rhino, d'un Land Raider ou, dans le cas de ces Tactical Squads, d'un Drop Pod.

Gegenüber: Jede Einheit der Armee hat ein angeschlossenes Transportfahrzeug, sei es ein Rhino, Land Raider oder, wie bei diesen Tactical Squads, ein Drop Pod.

"I've painted all the weapon options for my Dreadnoughts," says Ben. "It means I can equip them differently for each battle." This Dreadnought is equipped with deadly mortis autocannons to take down enemy flyers.

"J'ai peint toutes les options d'armes pour mes Dreadnoughts," explique Ben. "Je peux ainsi les configurer pour chaque bataille." Ce Dreadnought est équipé d'autocanons Mortis, pour abattre les aéronefs ennemis.

„Ich habe alle Waffenoptionen für meine Dreadnoughts bemalt", sagt Ben. „So kann ich sie in jeder Schlacht anders ausrüsten." Dieser Dreadnought ist mit Mortis-Maschinenkanonen gegen Flieger bestückt.

This Dreadnought is a Mk. IV resin Dreadnought from Forge World. Ben used an etched-brass Chapter symbol from Forge World on the Dreadnought's sarcophagus alongside transfers and freehand markings on its greaves.

Cette figurine est un Dreadnought Mk. IV Forge World en résine. Ben a appliqué sur le sarcophage un symbole de chapitre en photodécoupe Forge World ainsi que des décalques et des motifs à main levée sur ses jambières.

Dieser Dreadnought ist ein Typ-VI-Dreadnought aus Resin von Forge World. Ben verwendete ein Messing-Ätzteil des Ordenssymbols von Forge World auf dem Sarcophagus, Abziehbilder und freihändige Malereien auf den Beinschienen.

"I painted my Red Scorpions in a simple and effective colour scheme," adds Ben, "one that I could replicate easily over dozens of models and that wouldn't be too time-consuming. I had a lot of models to paint, after all!"

"J'ai peint mes Red Scorpions dans un schéma simple et efficace," ajoute Ben, "afin de pouvoir le reproduire facilement sur des dizaines de figurines sans y passer trop de temps. Après tout, j'en avais un paquet à peindre !"

„Ich bemalte meine Red Scorpions in einem einfachen und effektiven Farbschema", sagt Ben, „in einem, das ich leicht auf Dutzende Modelle auftragen konnte und nicht lange dauerte. Ich musste ja eine Menge malen."

"Each model is basecoated with Mechanicus Standard Grey, washed with Nuln Oil and drybrushed with lighter greys – that's it. I didn't edge highlight any of the models as I wanted them to look dirty and gritty rather than pristine."

"En fait, chaque figurine reçoit une couche de base de Mechanicus Standard Grey, un lavis de Nuln Oil et des brossages à sec en gris clairs. Je n'ai éclairci les arêtes d'aucune figurine car je les voulais réalistes et salies, pas immaculées."

„Jedes Modell erhielt eine Grundschicht Mechanicus Standard Grey, getuscht mit Nuln Oil und trocken-gebürstet mit helleren Grautönen. Ich akzentuier-te die Kanten nicht, weil ich wollte, dass sie abgenutzt aussehen."

This Legion Fellblade is the pride of Ben's force. He used Forge World weathering powders to give it a muddy appearance.

Ce Legion Fellblade est la fierté de la force de Ben. Il a utilisé les pigments Forge World pour le salir.

Dieser Legion Fellblade ist der Stolz von Bens Armee. Er verwendete Forge World Weathering Powders, um ihn matschig aussehen zu lassen.

The hull of Ben's Fellblade is covered in purity seals, litanies and scripture. The doors featuring the Chapter symbol are also available from Forge World.

La coque du Fellblade de Ben est couverte de sceaux de pureté, d'inscriptions et de litanies. Les portes avec icône de chapitre proviennent également de chez Forge World.

Der Rumpf von Bens Fellblade ist bedeckt mit Reinheitsiegeln, Litaneien und Schriften. Die Türen mit dem Ordenssymbol sind bei Forge World erhältlich.

Ben used a sponge and Forge World's weathering powders to apply chipped paintwork to his vehicles. Useful painting tips like this can be found in the Forge World Model Masterclass books.

Ben a utilisé une éponge et des pigments Forge World pour réaliser des effets de peinture éraflée sur ses véhicules. Des astuces de ce genre sont données dans les livres Model Masterclass Forge World.

Ben verwendete einen Schwamm und Forge World Weathering Powders, um abgeplatzten Lack darzustellen. Tipps wie diesen findest du in den „Model Masterclass"-Büchern von Forge World.

Carab Culln (seen on the right) is the Lord High Commander of the Red Scorpions Chapter and the leader of Ben's army. Below you can see his bodyguard of Terminators emerging from the dark depths of their Land Raider Crusader, ready to bring death to the Chapter's foes.

Carab Culln (à droite) est le Lord High Commander du chapitre des Red Scorpions et le chef de l'armée de Ben. Ci-dessous se trouve sa suite de Terminators qui émerge des profondeurs de son Land Raider Crusader, prête à apporter la mort aux ennemis du chapitre.

Carab Culln (rechts) ist der Lord High Commander des Ordens der Red Scorpions und der Anführer von Bens Armee. Unten kannst du sehen, wie seine Terminatorleibgarde aus ihrem Land Raider Crusader steigt, bereit, den Feinden ihres Ordens den Tod zu bringen.

Ben has painted ten Captains, one for each company of the Red Scorpions Chapter (and a possible indication of what he intends to paint in the future…). The two on the left are website exclusive models that were released to celebrate the new Games Workshop website.

Ben a peint dix capitaines, un pour chaque compagnie du chapitre des Red Scorpions (et une possible indication sur ce qu'il projette de peindre…). Les deux ci-contre sont des figurines en exclusivité Web sorties pour fêter le nouveau site Internet de Games Workshop.

Ben bemalte zehn Captains, einen für jede Company der Red Scorpions (vielleicht ein Hinweis auf das, was er noch bemalen will). Die beiden links wurden zur Feier der neuen Games-Workshop-Website veröffentlicht und waren dort exklusiv erhältlich.

Every model in Ben's army is converted in some way. "I take great pains to ensure that no two models look the same," says Ben. "I use adhesive putty to dry-fit all my models before applying any glue. That way I can make sure their poses look natural and believable."

Chaque figurine de l'armée de Ben est convertie d'une façon ou d'une autre. "Je veille à ce que toutes mes figurines soient uniques," précise Ben. "J'utilise de la pâte adhésive pour monter mes figurines avant d'utiliser de la colle. Ainsi je m'assure que leurs postures ont l'air naturelles et crédibles."

Jedes Modell in Bens Armee ist umgebaut. „Ich gebe mir Mühe, dass kein Modell aussieht wie das andere", sagt er. „Ich verwende Knetmasse und prüfe die Passung der Modelle, bevor ich Kleber benutze. So kann ich für natürliche und glaubhafte Posen sorgen."

Ben's force features a large contingent of bikes, including a Command Squad on bikes so he can field an entirely mounted army. Like all the units in his army, every squad includes an Apothecary, a unique Chapter trait to ensure the purity of their geneseed.

La force de Ben comprend un contingent de motards, dont une Command Squad afin de pouvoir aligner une armée complète à moto. Comme toutes les unités de son armée, chaque escouade comprend un Apothecary, un trait de chapitre unique veillant à la pureté de leur patrimoine génétique.

Bens Armee enthält ein großes Kontingent Bikes, inklusive eines Command Squads, sodass er eine komplett motorisierte Armee aufstellen kann. Wie alle Einheiten seiner Armee enthalten diese Squads einen Apothecary, der die Gensaat der Red Scorpions rein hält.

Aside from their large number of Apothecaries, the Red Scorpions follow the Codex Astartes closely. This Relic Contemptor Dreadnought clearly has a Chapter Veteran interred within it, as shown by the suit's white helmet and the heraldic shield mounted on its left shoulder.

Mis à part leur grand nombre d'Apothecaries, les Red Scorpions suivent le Codex Astartes à la lettre. Ce Relic Contemptor Dreadnought abrite clairement un vétéran du chapitre, comme l'indiquent son casque blanc et l'écu héraldique sur son épaule gauche.

Von ihren vielen Apothecaries abgesehen, folgen die Red Scorpions dem Codex Astartes. In diesem Relic Contemptor Dreadnought wurde ein Veteran des Ordens beigesetzt, erkennbar am weißen Helm und dem heraldischen Schild auf seiner linken Schulter.

The artisans of the Red Scorpions are master craftsmen and the Chapter maintains a large number of ancient relics and war machines, such as this Deredeo pattern Dreadnought. A mark of its Veteran status can be seen by the faded Crux Terminatus on its knee.

Les artisans des Red Scorpions sont des maîtres de leur art et le chapitre entretient un grand nombre de reliques tel ce Dreadnought Deredeo. La Crux Terminatus à demi effacée sur la genouillère atteste du statut de vétéran du frère incarcéré dans le marcheur.

Die Handwerker der Red Scorpions sind Meister ihres Fachs und der Orden unterhält eine große Zahl an Reliquien und Kriegsmaschinen wie diesen Deredeo-Dreadnought. Seinen Veteranenstatus erkennt man am ausgeblichenen Crux Terminatus auf seinem Knie.

Ben's Master of the Forge is surrounded by servo skulls mounted on flying stands to make them look like they're floating around him The Dreadnought to the left is an ironclad, its arms equipped with siege drills, claws and flamers for tearing apart enemy fortifications.

Le Maître de la Forge de Ben est entouré de servo-crânes sur tiges transparentes pour leur donner l'impression de flotter autou de lui. Le Dreadnought ci-contre est un Ironclad, aux bras équipés de foreuses de siège, de griffes et de lance-flammes pour raser les fortifications ennemies.

Bens Master of the Forge ist umgeben von Servoschädeln auf Flugbases, die aussehen, als ob sie schweben. Der Dreadnought links ist ausgerüste mit Belagerungsbohrern, Klauen und Flammenwerfern mit denen er feindliche Befestigungen einreißen kann.

The Red Scorpions favour full-on frontal assaults, which is why this Storm Eagle Gunship is heavily battle-damaged from centuries of constant warfare.

Les Red Scorpions favorisent les assauts frontaux, c'est pourquoi ce Storm Eagle Gunship porte les stigmates de siècles de guerre constante.

Die Red Scorpions greifen am liebsten frontal an, weshalb dieses Storm Eagle Gunship durch Jahrhunderte der Kriegsführung schwer beschädigt ist.

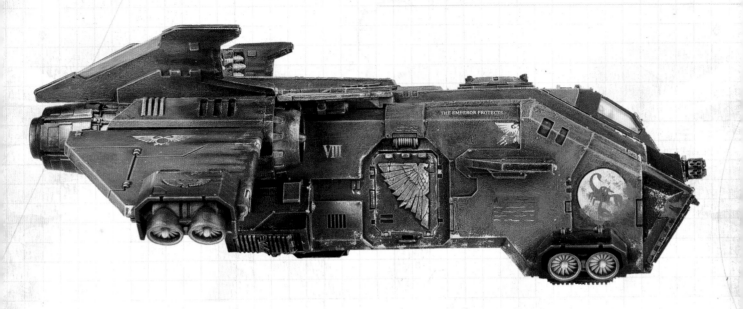

The yellow on Ben's models was painted as efficiently as the rest of the colours on his models. "I used Averland Sunset, washed with Seraphim Sepia and highlighted with Yriel Yellow. Simple."

Le jaune des figurines de Ben a été peint aussi efficacement que les autres couleurs. "J'ai utilisé de l'Averland Sunset, avec un lavis de Seraphim Sepia, le tout éclairci avec de l'Yriel Yellow. Simple."

Das Gelb auf Bens Modellen wurde so effizient gemalt wie der Rest der Farben auf seinen Modellen. „Ich verwendete Averland Sunset, tuschte mit Seraphim Sepia und akzentuierte mit Yriel Yellow."

Ben has made good use of Forge World armour sets, taking individual components from them and combining them with plastic kits. None of the parts go to waste, though, a great example of how versatile and compatible Space Marine kits are.

Ben a fait bon usage des sets d'armures Forge World, en combinant des éléments individuels avec des kits plastique. Aucun composant n'a été gâché, preuve de la grande adaptabilité et de la compatibilité des kits de la gamme Space Marine.

Ben hat die Rüstungssets von Forge World sinnvoll verwendet und Teile von ihnen mit Kunststoffbausätzen kombiniert. Kein Teil ging verloren, ein tolles Beispiel dafür, wie vielseitig und kompatibel Space-Marine-Bausätze sind.

The Masters of the Chapter set make up four of Ben's commanders. From left to right they are the Master of Recruits, Master of the Arsenal, Master of the Fleet and Master of the watch. They have all been subtly converted with either iron halos or back banners.

Le set de Masters of the Chapter a fourni quatre des commandants de Ben. De gauche à droite se trouvent le Maître des Recrues, le Maître de l'Arsenal, le Maître de la Flotte, et le Maître du Guet. Tous ont été convertis avec un halo de fer ou une bannière.

Das Set „Meister des Ordens" stellt vier von Bens Befehlshabern. Von links nach rechts: Meister der Rekruten, Meister des Arsenals, Meister der Flotte und Meister der Wache. Sie alle wurden mit Stählernen Sternen oder Bannern leicht umgebaut.

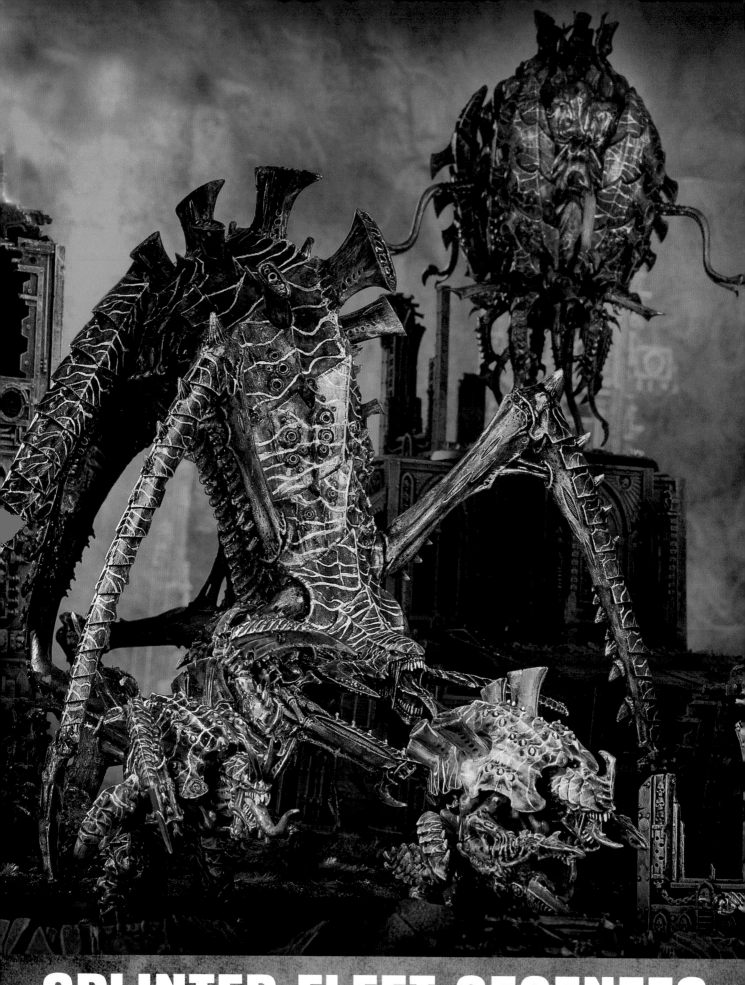

SPLINTER FLEET GEGENEES

The ravenous Tyranids of Splinter Fleet Gegenees are the brain-child of Tom Harrison, a monstrous invasion of teeth, claws and unnatural appendages.

Les tyranids voraces de la vrille Gegenees ont été enfantés par Tom Harrison, telle une monstrueuse invasion de dents, de griffes et d'appendices anormaux.

Die Tyraniden von Splitterflotte Gegenees sind die Schöpfung von Tom Harrison, eine monströse Invasion aus Zähnen, Klauen und unnatürlichen Gliedern.

Tom's collection is almost entirely made up of monstrous creatures like this hulking Tyrannofex.

La collection de Tom n'inclut presque que des créatures monstrueuses, comme ce Tyrannofex.

Toms Sammlung besteht fast ausschließlich aus monströsen Kreaturen wie diesem Tyrannofex.

The colour scheme was achieved by applying lots of different Shades directly over a Corax White undercoat.

Ce shéma de couleurs est obtenu en appliquant beaucoup de Shades sur une sous-couche de Corax White undercoat.

Das Farbschema erzeugte er mit Schichten verschiedener Shades direkt auf einer Grundierung mit Corax White.

This Tyrannocyte has been cunningly converted to float upside-down, its body covered in bio-weapons.

Ce Tyrannocyte a été astucieusement converti pour flotter la tête en bas, son corps couvert de bio-armes.

Dieser Tyrannocyte wurde raffiniert kopfüber schwebend gebaut und starrt vor Biowaffen.

The fleshy areas are painted using several washes of Carroburg Crimson and Reikland Fleshshade to give it a raw, skinless appearance.

Les zones de chair sont peintes avec plusieurs lavis de Carroburg Crimson et de Reikland Fleshshade pour donner un aspect brut et écorché.

Die Fleischbereiche wurden mehrmals mit Carroburg Crimson und Reikland Fleshshade getuscht, um rau und hautlos auszusehen.

A Hierophant bio-titan, the largest model in Tom's collection. Despite its size, it was still painted using the same techniques as Tom's other models.

Un bio-titan Hierophant, la plus grande figurine de la collection de Tom. Malgré sa taille, il a été peint de la même façon que ses autres figurines.

Ein Hierophant-Biotitan, das größte Modell der Sammlung. Trotz der Größe bemalte Tom ihn mit denselben Techniken wie die anderen Modelle.

The mottled carapace was achieved by applying washes of Biel-Tan Green and Athonian Camoshade, which were allowed to mix as they dried.

L'apparence mouchetée de la carapace a été obtenue en appliquant des lavis d'Athonian Camoshade et de Biel-Tan Green, qui se sont mélangés en séchant.

Den fleckigen Panzer erreichte er mit mehreren Tuscheschichten Biel-Tan Green und Athonian Camoshade, die sich beim Trocknen vermengten.

The carapace striations were painted using White Scar, followed by a selective wash of Seraphim Sepia over the whole model. Tom didn't worry about being too neat, his logic being that the carapace and flesh would naturally merge in places.

Les stries de la carapace ont été peintes en White Scar, suivi d'un lavis sélectif de Seraphim Sepia sur toute la figurine. Tom ne s'est pas soucié de netteté, sa logique étant que la carapace et la chair fusionnent à certains endroits.

Die Streifen auf dem Panzer malte er mit White Scar auf und tuschte dann selektiv mit Seraphim Sepia Bereiche am ganzen Modell. Tom achtete nicht zu sehr auf Sorgfalt, denn er sieht es als logisch an, das Fleisch und Panzer hier und da verschmelzen.

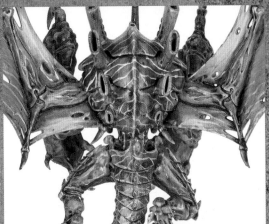

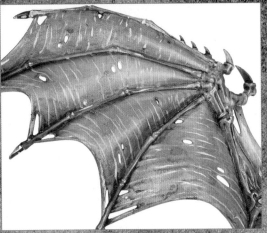

This flying Hive Tyrant has been converted with a spare pair of arms from the Tyrannofex kit. The blue ribbing on its joints was painted with Nihilakh Oxide and glazed with Guilliman Blue to make it looks like otherworldly alien sinew.

Ce Hive Tyrant volant a été converti avec une paire de bras de Tyrannofex de rechange. Les nervures bleues ont été peintes en Nihilakh Oxide avant de recevoir un glacis de Guilliman Blue pour leur donner une apparence de tendons extraterrestres.

Der fliegende Schwarmtyrant wurde mit einem Armpaar des Tyrannofex-Bausatzes umgebaut. Das Blau um die Flügelknochen malte er mit Nihilakh Oxide und lasierte es mit Guilliman Blue, um den Eindruck andersweltlicher Sehnen zu erzeugen.

THE COHORT OF KANISH

This mighty Necron army was painted by collector and painter Ben Johnson. Ben built the army up over several months as part of an ongoing series of articles titled 'Call to Arms'. We're proud to present it here in all its glory!

Cette redoutable armée de necrons est l'œuvre de Ben Johnson, peintre et grand collectionneur. Ben a bâti cette armée au fil des mois au cours d'une série d'articles intitulée "Call to Arms". Nous sommes fiers de vous la présenter dans toute sa gloire !

Diese mächtige Necron-Armee wurde vom Sammler und Maler Ben Johnson bemalt. Ben baute die Armee über mehrere Monate im Zuge einer Artikelreihe namens „Call to Arms" auf. Wir freuen uns, sie hier in all ihrer Pracht präsentieren zu können!

Ben often kit-bashes his models to make unique items for his collection. This Aegis Defence Line as been given a distinctly Necron feel with lots of spare parts.

Ben mélange souvent les kits pour obtenir des pièces uniques. Cette Aegis Defence Line a reçu une saveur necron grâce à l'ajout de nombreuses pièces de rechange.

Ben kit-basht Modelle häufig, um für seine Sammlung Einzelstücke zu erschaffen. Diese Aegis-Verteidigungslinie wirkt durch viele überzählige Teile necronartig.

Ben paints at an astonishing speed, which is just as well – he concocted a labour-intensive 16-stage system for painting the Necron Warriors in his army.

Ben peint à une vitesse hallucinante sans sacrifier sur le rendu – il a concocté une méthode intensive en 16 étapes pour peindre les Necron Warriors de son armée.

Ben malt unglaublich schnell, was gut ist – er hat ein 16-stufiges arbeitsintensives Bemalsystem für die Necron Warriors seiner Armee ausgearbeitet.

Destroyer Lords are Ben's favourite Necrons, so he converted Kanish the Evermore to lead his army, a model based on an illustration by John Blanche.

Les Destroyer Lords sont les necrons favoris de Ben, qui a converti Kanish the Evermore pour mener son armée, une figurine inspirée d'une illustration de John Blanche.

Destroyer Lords sind Bens Lieblinge, weswegen er nach einer Illustration von John Blanche Kanish the Evermore als Anführer seiner Armee umbaute.

The Cryptek watches on as phalanxes of Necron Warriors and Immortals march resolutely into battle. An Annihilation Barge provides formidable fire support.

Le Cryptek veille comme des phalanges de Necron Warriors et d'Immortals marchent résolument au combat. Une Annihilation Barge fournit un soutien redoutable.

Der Cryptek passt auf, als Phalangen aus Necron Warriors und Immortals entschlossen in die Schlacht ziehen. Eine Annihilation Barge liefert Feuerunterstützung.

The Doom Scythe is an aerial horror, capable of obliterating tanks and men alike with its death ray.

Le Doom Scythe est une horreur volante, capable d'oblitérer chars et soldats avec son rayon de mort.

Die Doom Scythe ist ein Schrecken der Lüfte und löscht mit dem Todesstrahl Panzer wie Männer aus.

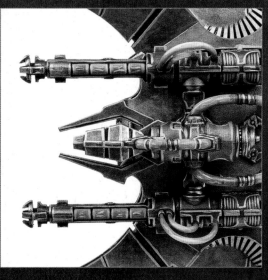

Ben added a little colour to his Doom Scythe with some blue glazing in the recesses. The weapons underneath have the same green energy glow you can see throughout his army – he even repainted the little transparent rods in the gauss weapons.

Ben a ajouté un peu de couleurs à son Doom Scythe avec des glacis bleus dans les creux. Les armes sous le ventre ont le même halo verdâtre que sur toute l'armée – Ben a même repeint les petits bâtons transparents verts des armes Gauss.

Ben fügte seiner Doom Scythe mit blauer Lasur in den Vertiefungen etwas Farbe hinzu. Die Waffen darunter weisen das grüne Glühen auf, dass du bei der ganzen Armee siehst – er hat sogar die transparenten Stäbe der Gauss-waffen umgemalt.

Ben likes modelling his flyers (and flying creatures for Warhammer Age of Sigmar) so you can't see the flying stand. This Doom Scythe appears to be skimming just over the shoulder of the Space Marine statue from the Honoured Imperium kit.

Ben aime bricoler ses aéronefs (et les créatures volantes de Warhammer Age of Sigmar) pour camoufler leur tige de support. Ce Doom Scythe semble voler juste au-dessus de l'épaule de la statue space marine du kit Honoured Imperium.

Ben baut Flieger (und fliegende Kreaturen für Warhammer Age of Sigmar) gerne so, dass man das Flugbase nicht sieht. Diese Doom Scythe scheint über der Schulter der Space-Marine-Statue des Ehrwürdiges-Imperium-Bausatzes zu schweben.

The Lychguard compete for the honour of being Ben's favourite unit in the army. He loves the deathly aspect of them as they lay waste to the enemy with warscythes.

Les Lychguard luttent pour l'honneur d'être l'unité préférée de Ben dans cette armée. Il adore leur aspect létal comme ils ravagent l'ennemi à coup de fauchards.

Die Lychguard konkurriert um die Ehre als Bens Lieblingseinheit der Armee. Er mag ihre tödliche Art, mit der sie den Gegner mit Kriegssensen verheeren.

The C'tan Shard of the Nightbringer is one of the true centrepieces of the collection. Ben likes to invite his opponent to draw the card to see which power he unleashes!

Le C'tan Shard of the Nightbringer est une des pièces centrale de cette collection. Ben adore inviter son adversaire à tirer les cartes pour savoir quels pouvoirs il va déchaîner!

Der C'tan Shard of the Nightbringer ist ein wahres Kernstück der Sammlung. Ben lädt seinen Gegner gerne ein, die Karte der Kraft zu ziehen, die er entfesselt.

GOLDEN DEMON: TANKS

We continue our coverage of Golden Demon: Tanks from Warhammer World in 2015.

Nous poursuivons notre couverture du Golden Demon : Tanks qui eut lieu à Warhammer World en 2015.

Fortsetzung unser Berichterstattung über den Golden Demon: Tanks in der Warhammer World 2015.

Solar Auxilia Leman Russ by Paul Robins. Single Tank category. Paul has built up layers of grease and grime in the recesses for a hard-worn appearance.

Leman Russ Solar Auxilia par Paul Robins. Catégorie Char individuel. Paul a accumulé les couches de crasse dans les creux pour obtenir un aspect usé.

Solar Auxilia Leman Russ von Paul Robins. Kategorie „Single Tank". Paul ließ den Panzer durch Ölreste und Dreck in den Vertiefungen sehr abgenutzt wirken.

Eldar Warp Hunter by John Beech. Single Tank category. We interviewed John about this amazing entry in White Dwarf 90.

Warp Hunter Eldar par John Beech. Catégorie Char individuel. Nous avons interviewé John à propos de cette entrée fantastique dans White Dwarf 90.

Eldar Warp Hunter von John Beech. Kategorie „Single Tank". Wir führten in White Dwarf 90 ein Interviw mit John über seinen faszinierenden Beitrag.

We were gobsmacked when we saw this hovering Eldar grav tank – John has made use of small electro-magnets to have it levitate above its base.

Nous avons été abasourdis en voyant ce char antigrav eldar – John a utilisé de petits électroaimants pour le faire léviter au-dessus de son socle.

Wir konnten es kaum glauben, als wir diesen schwebenden Eldar-Grav-panzer sahen. John nutze kleine Elektromagneten, um ihn schweben zu lassen.

Vostroyan Macharius tank by Kristian
Simonsen. Bronze, Unbound category.

Char Macharius Vostroyan par Kristian
Simonsen. Bronze, catégorie Libre.

Vostroyanischer Macharius von Kristian
Simonsen. Bronze, Kategorie „Unbound".

Kristian has executed an exquisite paint-job, making the hull of his Macharius look chipped, scuffed and caked in layers of dirt, grime and oily residue.

Kristian a exécuté un travail de peinture très poussé, la coque de son Macharius semblant éraflée et couverte de poussière, de crasse et de résidus graisseux.

Kristian hat den Macharius exzellent bemalt, indem er seinen Rumpf mit Kratzern, Abplatzungen und Ablagerungen aus Staub, Dreck und Öl bedeckte.

The churned up mud of the scenic base is incredibly realistic, complete with rusting detritus and filthy puddles. Kristian has even splattered the mud up the tracks and hull.

La boue du socle scénique est incroyablement réaliste, incrustée de résidus rouillés et de flaques troubles. Kristian a été jusqu'à enduire de boue les chenilles et le bas de caisse de son char.

Der zerwühlte Schlamm des szenischen Bases ist unglaublich realistisch mit rostigen Überresten und Dreckpfützen. Kristian spritzte sogar Schlamm auf Ketten und Rumpf.

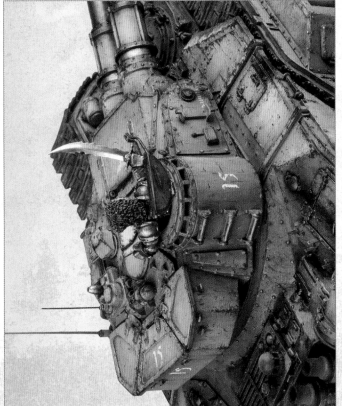

Death Guard Legion Fellblade by Richard Gray. Gold, Single Tank category and Slayer Sword Winner.

Legion Fellblade Death Guard par Richard Gray. Or, catégorie Char Individuel et vainqueur de la Slayer Sword.

Death Guard Legion Fellblade von Richard Gray. Gold, Kategorie „Single Tank" und Slayer-Sword-Gewinner.

A close inspection of Richard's Fellblade makes it clear why he won the Slayer Sword: amazing freehand markings, realistic weathering (look at all that rust!) and incredible attention to detail.

Un examen rapproché du Fellblade de Richard explique pourquoi il a remporté la Slayer Sword : magnifiques dessins à main levée, salissures réalistes (regardez la rouille !) et une minutie inouïe.

Die Großaufnahme zeigt deutlich, warum Richards Fellblade das Slayer Sword gewann: tolle Freihand-Makierungen, realistische Verwitterung (dieser Rost!) und ein unglaublicher Blick fürs Detail.

World Eaters Land Raider by Helge
Wilhelm Dahl. Single Tank category.

Land Raider World Eater par Helge
Wilhelm Dahl. Catégorie Char Individuel.

World Eaters Land Raider von Helge
Wilhelm Dahl. Kategorie „Single Tank".

Around the Land Raider lie dead Ultramarines and World Eaters, their bodies broken and twisted in the churned mud.

Autour du Land Raider gisent Ultramarines et World Eaters, leurs corps brisés et tordus enfoncés dans la boue retournée.

Rings um den Land Raider liegen tote Ultramarines und World Eaters, deren verdrehte Leiber im Schlamm versinken.

The hull of this Land Raider has been blasted by war. In places the paintwork has been scratched to the bare metal beneath.

La coque de ce Land a été Raider rongée par la guerre. Par endroits, la peinture a été arrachée jusqu'à mettre le métal à nu.

Der Rumpf dieses Land Raider ist vom Krieg gezeichnet. An einigen Stellen sieht man das freigelegte Metall.

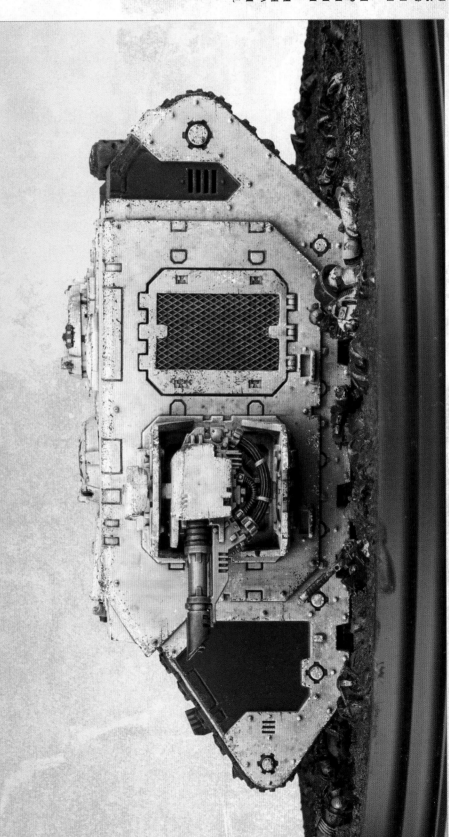

Imperial Fists Legion
Sicarian Squadron by Andy
Wardle. Bronze, Tank
Squadron category.

Escadron de Legion Sicarian
Imperial Fists par Andy
Wardle. Bronze, Catégorie
Escadron de Chars.

Imperial Fists Legion
Sicarian Squadron von Andy
Wardle. Bronze, Kategorie
„Tank Squadron".

Spear

Andy's paint-job includes
some amazing freehand,
with Imperial Fists
iconography adorning the
hulls of both tanks.

La peinture d'Andy inclut
des dessins à main levée
fantastiques, l'iconographie
des Imperial Fists ornant
les coques des deux chars.

Zu Andys Bemalung
gehören auch tolle
Freihandmalereien mit
Ikonographie der Imperial
Fists auf den Rümpfen.

The scuffs and weathering on this squadron help to balance the otherwise bright yellow armour.

Sur cet escadron, éraflures et salissures contribuent à abaisser l'intensité du jaune de leur blindage.

Kratzer und Verwitterung brechen bei dieser Schwadron optisch das strahlende Gelb auf.

f Dorn

The bright yellow armour plates have a gradated blend from dark to light, an amazing technique to use across the whole model.

Les plaques jaune vif ont été fondues du sombre au clair, une technique incroyable, employée sur la figurine entière.

Das Gelb der Panzerung ist überall von Dunkel zu Hell geschichtet, eine tolle Technik, die am ganzen Modell genutzt wurde.

Death Korps of Krieg Macharius
Vanquisher by Andrew McGee.
Single Tank category.

Macharius Vanquisher Death Korps
of Krieg par Andrew McGee.
Catégorie Char Individuel.

Macharius Vanquisher des Todeskorps von
Krieg, bemalt von Andrew McGee.
Kategorie „Single Tank".

The drab green of this Macharius tank's paint scheme reflects the dour nature of the Death Korps, a regiment known for its morbid outlook.

Le vert morne du schéma de couleurs de ce char Macharius reflète la nature glauque des Death Korps, un régiment connu pour son apparence morbide.

Das matte Grün dieses Macharius-Panzers passt zum düsteren Wesen des Todeskorps von Krieg, das für sein morbides Äußeres bekannt ist.

Andy has included simple vehicle markings on his tank, an off-white stripe and numerals – which looks like they been eroded by the harsh environment.

Andy a ajouté de simples marquages à son char, une bande blanche avec un numéro, qui semblent avoir été érodés par un environnement difficile.

Andy hat einfache Fahrzeug-markierungen an diesem Panzer verwendet, streifen mit Zahlen, die aussehen, wie von der harten Umgebung gezeichnet.

The *Hidden Hunter*, Legion Sicaran Venator by Raymond Hale. Unbound category.

The *Hidden Hunter*, Legion Sicaran Venator par Raymond Hale. Catégorie Libre.

The *Hidden Hunter*, Legion Sicaran Venator von Raymond Hale. Kategorie „Unbound".

Lurking amid the ruins, a Sicaran Venator lines up a kill shot. We love the pustules impossibly bulging through the thick armour of the tank.

Rôdant parmi les ruines, un Sicaran Venator ajuste un tir fatal. Nous adorons les pustules bourgeonnant de façon impossible à travers l'épais blindage du char.

Ein Sicaran Venator lauert inmitten von Ruinen auf den Fangschuß. Wir lieben die Pusteln, die sich bizarrer Weise durch die dicken Panzerung drücken.

Ultramarines Land Raider
by Naomi North. Single
Tank category.

Land Raider Ultramarine
par Naomi North. Catégorie
Char Individuel.

Ultramarines Land Raider
von Naomi North.
Kategorie „Single Tank".

Black Legion Spartan
Assault Tank by Raymond
Hale. Single Tank category.

Spartan Assault Tank Black
Legion par Raymond Hale.
Catégorie Char Individuel.

Black Legion Spartan Assault
Tank von Raymond Hale.
Kategorie „Single Tank".

Renegade Malcador
Defender by Helge
Wilhelm Dahl. Unbound
category.

Malcador Defender
renégat par Helge
Wilhelm Dahl.
Catégorie Libre.

Renegade Malcador
Defender von Helge
Wilhelm Dahl. Kategorie
„Unbound".

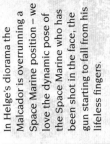

In Helge's diorama the Malcador is overrunning a Space Marine position – we love the dynamic pose of the Space Marine who has been shot in the face, the gun starting to fall from his lifeless fingers.

Dans le diorama de Helge, le Malcador déborde une position space marine – nous adorons le dynamisme du space marine touché au visage, et dont le bolter glisse des doigts désormais sans vie.

In Helges Diorama überwindet der Malcador eine Position der Space Marines – wir lieben die Dynamik des Space Marines, dem ins Gesicht geschossen wurde und dem die Waffe aus den leblosen Händen fällt.

CHILDREN OF THE STARS

From beyond the stars they came: a Seraphon constellation painted by starmaster Amy Snuggs.

D'au-delà des étoiles ils vinrent, une constellation de seraphons peints par le starmaster Amy Snuggs.

Von jenseits der Sterne stammt diese Seraphon-Constellation, bemalt von Starmaster Amy Snuggs.

Amy was inspired to start a Seraphon army following the release of Warhammer Age of Sigmar. "It was the vibrant colours, exciting painting opportunities and fantastical monsters that encouraged me to collect them," says Amy.

Amy a été poussée à commencer une armée de seraphons avec la sortie de Warhammer Age of Sigmar. "Leurs couleurs vives, les possibilités de peinture et leurs monstres fantastiques m'ont encouragé à entamer leur collection," confie Amy.

Amy wurde durch Warhammer Age of Sigmar zu einer Seraphon-Armee inspiriert. „Die kräftigen Farben, spannenden Bemalmöglichkeiten und fantastischen Monster brachten mich dazu, sie zu sammeln", erzählt Amy.

Lord Kroak is the leader of Amy's force. He proved his magical skills at a recent Age of Sigmar campaign day where Amy won the award for best-painted army.

Lord Kroak est le chef de la force d'Amy. Il prouva son talent de mage lors d'une récente campagne d'Age of Sigmar où amy remporta le prix de la plus belle armée.

Lord Kroak führt Amys Armee an. Er bewies kürzlich in einer „Age of Sigmar"-Kampagne sein Geschick, bei der Amy den Award für die am besten bemalte Armee gewann.

"I wanted my Seraphon to be dark-skinned but vibrant," explains Amy, "which is why I used orange as their secondary colour and lots of bright spot colours."

"Je voulais des seraphons à peau sombre mais aux couleurs vives," explique Amy, "J'ai donc utilisé de l'orange comme teinte secondaire et plein de touches intenses."

„Ich wollte die Haut meiner Seraphon dunkel aber kräftig", erklärt Amy. „Daher benutzte ich Orange als Zweitfarbe und viele helle Schmuckfarben."

"The inspiration for my colour scheme was actually Vandus Hammerhand's Dracoth," says Amy. "Pretty much every colour on every model is drybrushed to give them a rough, lizard-like quality. I wanted my Seraphon to have a lot of texture in their colour scheme. I then used Shades to help tie the colours together."

"L'inspiration de mon schéma de couleur vient du Dracoth de Vandus Hammerhand," avoue Amy. "Les couleurs sont brossées à sec sur toutes les figurines pour un aspect rugueux et écailleux. Je voulais que mes seraphons aient beaucoup de textures dans leurs couleurs. J'ai ensuite utilisé des Shade pour lier les teintes."

„Tatsächlich inspirierte mich Vandus Hammerhands Dracoth zu diesem Farbschema. So gut wie jede Farbe habe ich trockengebürstet, damit sie rau und echsenartig wirken. Ich wollte viel Textur im Schmema meiner Seraphon haben. Anschließend benutzte ich Shades um die Farben miteinander zu verbinden."

The orange stripes on
Amy's Seraphon war-beasts
were inspired by the
Scar-Veteran on Carnosaur
that was painted by the
Studio's army painters.
The stripe is three
drybrushed layers of
Jokaero Orange, Troll Slaye
Orange and Lugganath
Orange followed by a wash
of Fuegan Orange and a
glaze of Casandora Yellow.

Les bandes orange sur les
monstres seraphons d'Amy
ont été inspirées par le
Scar-Veteran sur Carnosaur
réalisé par les peintres
d'armée du Studio. Les
bandes sont brossées en
Jokaero Orange, puis en
Troll Slayer Orange et enfir
en Lugganath Orange suivi
d'un lavis de Fuegan
Orange et d'un glacis
de Casandora Yellow.

Die orangen Streifen auf
den Kriegsbestien sind
vom Scar-Veteran auf
Carnosaur unserer
Studio-Armeebemaler
inspiriert. Ein Streifen
besteht aus drei trockenge
bürsteten Schichten aus
Jokaero Orange, Troll Slaye
Orange und Lugganath
Orange sowie einer Lasur
mit Casandora Yellow.

"...think the Dread Saurian is probably my favourite model in the army," says Amy. "It's just so huge and impressive! It formed the centrepiece for my Armies on Parade entry this year."

"...Je pense que le Dread Saurian est ma figurine préférée de cette armée," précise Amy. "Il est tellement impressionnant ! Il a constitué la pièce centrale de mon plateau Armies on Parade cette année."

„...Ich denke, der Dread Saurian ist wohl mein Lieblingsmodell der Armee", sagt Amy. „Es ist so groß und eindrucksvoll! Dieses Jahr bei Armies on Parade war es der Blickfang meiner Armee."

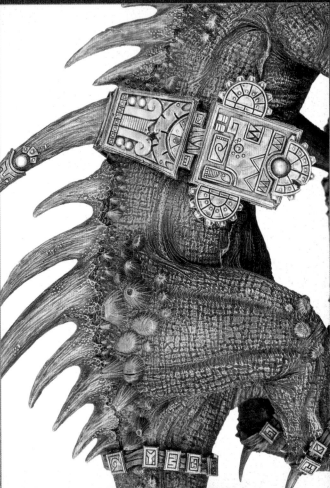

"I found watching the painting videos on the Games Workshop website really helpful when learning to paint," says Amy who, perhaps unbelievably, has only been painting for a year.

« J'ai trouvé les vidéos du site Games Workshop d'un grand secours pour apprendre à peindre, » révèle Amy qui, même si cela peut sembler difficile à croire, ne peint que depuis un an.

„Ich fand die Bemalvideos auf der Website von Games Workshop sehr hilfreich beim Lernen, wie man gut bemalt", sagt Amy, die – kaum zu glauben – erst seit einem Jahr bemalt.

This Troglodon really stands out from the rest of the army, an albino amongst dark-skinned saurians. It retains the same orange markings, though.

Ce Troglodon se détache du reste de l'armée, un albinos au milieu de sauriens à la peau sombre. Toutefois, il conserve les mêmes marquages orange.

Dieser Troglodon sticht als Albino unter dunklen Saurus natürlich aus der Armee hervor. Er hat jedoch dieselben orangen Markierungen.

"I intend to have one of every Seraphon model in my army," laughs Amy. "It's a collection and I want it to be complete. I can then pick and choose what I want for each battle."

"Je compte avoir un exemplaire de chaque figurine de seraphon," dit Amy en riant, "pour avoir une collection complète. Je pourrais alors choisir ce que je veux à chaque bataille.

„Ich will jedes Seraphon-Modell einmal in meiner Armee haben", lacht Amy. „Ich will, dass die Sammlung vollständig ist. Dann kann ich für jede Schlacht die Richtigen wählen."

Many of Amy's Skink characters feature bright, almost luminous feathers to show their affinity with magic. The Saurus feature object source lighting around their weapons.

Les personnages Skinks d'Amy ont des plumes vives, quasi lumineuses pour montrer leur affinité avec la magie. Les Saurus ont un effet lumineux autour de leurs armes.

Viele ihrer Skink-Charakter-modelle haben helle, nahezu leuchtende Farben, die ihre Neigung zur Magie betonen. An den Waffen der Saurus arbeitete sie mit gerichteten Lichteffekten.

"Painting my Seraphon with lots of drybrushing was a really nice challenge," says Amy. "I've painted both Blood Angels and Skitarii over the last year and they're both quite neat armies – it was nice painting an army that was more organic."

"Peindre mes seraphons avec des brossages à sec était un défi agréable," confie Amy. "J'ai peint des Blood Angels et des Skitarii l'an passé et ce sont des armées assez nettes d'aspect – j'ai apprécié de peindre une armée plus organique."

„Seraphon mit viel Trockenbürsten zu bemalen war eine schöne Herausforderung. Ich habe im letzten Jahr Blood Angels und Skitarii bemalt, beides geordnete Armeen – es war schön, eine etwas organischere Armee zu bemalen."

Kroq-gar was one of the
first models Amy bought
for her collection, the
colour scheme almost
identical to the Studio one.
The Carnosaur's eyes are
painted bright green, a hint
at the celestial magic
coursing through its
monstrous body.

Kroq-gar fut l'une
des premières figurines
qu'Amy a achetée pour sa
collection, son schéma de
couleur presque identique
à celui du Studio. Les yeux
du Carnosaur sont peints
en vert vif suggérant la
magie céleste courant dans
son corps monstrueux.

Kroq-Gar gehörte zu den
ersten Modellen in Amys
Sammlung und sein
Farbschema ist beinahe
identisch mit dem des
Studios. Die Augen des
Carnosaurs sind leuchtend
grün bemalt, ein Hinweis
auf die celestische Energie,
die ihn durchströmt.

FIRST FOUNDING: ULTRAMARINES

In the first of a new series, we take a closer look at the First Founding Chapters of the Space Marines, beginning with the paragons of war, the Ultramarines.

Premier opus d'une nouvelle série, nous examinons les chapitres space marines de la Première Fondation, en commençant par les parangons de la guerre, les Ultramarines.

Im ersten Teil einer neuen Reihe betrachten wir die Orden der Ersten Gründung der Space Marines. Den Anfang machen die Vorzeigekrieger der Ultramarines.

The current Chapter Master of the Ultramarines is Marneus Calgar, the Lord Macragge. He is the epitome of his Chapter, a noble, fearless warrior who places the survival of the Imperium and its people above all else. He is armed with the relics known as the Gauntlets of Ultramar.

L'actuel Chapter Master des Ultramarines est Marneus Calgar, Lord Macragge. Il est la quintessence de son chapitre, un héros noble et sans peur plaçant la survie de l'Imperium et de son peuple au-dessus de tout. Il est armé d'une relique appelée les Gantelets de Ultramar.

Der gegenwärtige Chapter Master der Ultramarines ist Marneus Calgar, der Lord von Macragge. Er ist das Sinnbild seines Ordens, ein edler, furchtloser Krieger, der den Schutz des Imperiums und der Menschen darin über alles andere stellt. Er trägt die Fäuste von Ultramar.

Severus Agemman is the Chapter's First Captain and Regent of Ultramar. It falls to Agemman to rule over the Chapter's affairs when the Chapter Master is otherwise engaged, a duty that includes stewardship over more than 500 worlds on the Eastern Fringe of the Ultima Segmentum.

Severus Agemman est le Fist Captain du chapitre et Régent d'Ultramar. Il incombe à Agemman de régler les affaires du chapitre lorsque son maître est engagé ailleurs, une tâche qui inclut la gestion des quelque 500 mondes de la Bordure Orientale de l'Ultima Segmentum.

Severus Agemman ist Erster Captain des Ordens und Regent von Ultramar. Er hat das Kommando, wenn der Chapter Master anderweitig eingebunden ist. Diese Pflicht beinhaltet die Verwaltung von über 500 Welten im Östlichen Spiralarm des Segmentum Ultima.

Ortan Cassius is the Master of Sanctity, High Chaplain of the Ultramarines. At almost 400 years old, he is the oldest member of the Chapter, a heavily scarred veteran of the Tyrannic Wars. He has even commissioned a new unit to counter the alien threat: the Tyrannic War Veterans.

Ortan Cassius est le Maître de la Sainteté, le High Chaplain des Ultramarines. Âgé de presque 400 ans, il est le doyen du chapitre, un vétéran scarifié de la Première Guerre Tyrannique. Il a même constitué une nouvelle unité pour traiter la menace xenos : les Tyrannic War Veterans.

Ortan Cassius ist der Meister der Reinheit, der High Chaplain der Ultramarines. Mit fast 400 Jahren ist er der älteste des Ordens, ein vernarbter Veteran der Tyranidenkriege. Er hat sogar eine neue Einheit gegen die Xenos gegründet: Die Veteranen der Tyranidenkriege.

Varro Tigurius is the Chapter's Chief Librarian. A formidable psyker, his prescience has ensured the Ultramarines are always right where they're needed most. He is also the only human to have tapped into the Hive Mind of the Tyranids. He is tormented by what he saw…

Varro Tigurius est le Chief Librarian du chapitre. Psyker redoutable, sa prescience assure que les Ultramarines sont toujours où ils sont le plus attendus. Il est également le seul humain à avoir plongé dans l'Esprit-Ruche des tyranids. Il est depuis tourmenté par ce qu'il y a vu…

Varro Tigurius ist der Chief Librarian des Ordens, ein mächtiger Psioniker, dessen Voraussicht die Ultramarines immer dorthin bringt, wo sie gebraucht werden. Er ist auch der einzige Mensch, der ins Schwarmbewusstsein der Tyraniden geblickt hat. Es quält ihn bis heute …

The Codex Astartes was written by Roboute Guilliman, Primarch of the Ultramarines. His teachings and doctrines are followed by all members of the Chapter at all times.

Le Codex Astartes fut écrit par Roboute Guilliman, Primarch des Ultramarines. Ses enseignements et doctrines sont suivis par tous les membres du chapitre en permanence.

Roboute Guilliman, der Primarch der Ultramarines, schrieb den Codex Astartes. Alle Mitglieder des Ordens befolgen seine Lehren und Doktrinen ausnahmslos.

The Ultramarines march to war clad in blue power armour. They do not wear camouflage or disguise their livery, for it is a symbol of their honour, strength and courage.

Les Ultramarines marchent au combat en armures énergétiques bleue. Ils ne portent pas de camouflage ni ne maquillent leur livrée, car elle symbolise honneur, force et courage.

Die Ultramarines marschieren in blauer Servorüstung in den Krieg. Sie tragen keine Tarnung oder verbergen ihre Heraldik, denn sie ist Symbol ihrer Ehre, Stärke und Tapferkeit.

Cato Sicarius is the Captain of the Ultramarines 2nd Company and widely regarded as the finest swordsman in the Chapter. His most famous action to date is the war on Damnos, where he killed the Necron Overlord known as The Undying and reclaimed the planet for the Imperium.

Cato Sicarius est le Captain de la 2ᵉ Compagnie et il est considéré avec sagesse comme la plus fine lame de son chapitre. Son fait le plus illustre remonte à la guerre de Damnos, où il terrassa l'Overlord necron appelé The Undying et reconquit la planète au nom de l'Imperium.

Cato Sicarius ist Captain der 2. Company und als bester Schwertkämpfer des Ordens bekannt. Seine größte Tat war im Krieg auf Damnos, wo er den Necron Overlord tötete, der als der Unsterbliche bekannt war, und den Planeten für das Imperium zurückeroberte.

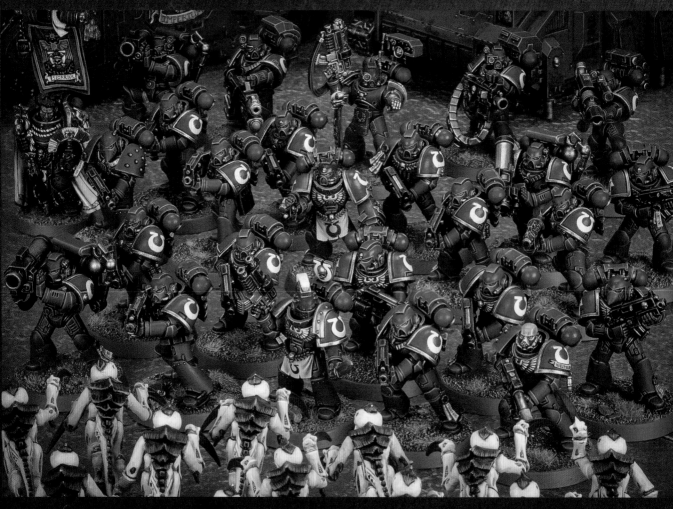

The Ultramarines follow the organisational structure of the Codex Astartes closely. This Tactical Squad have gold shoulder trims, indicating they belong to the 2nd Company.

Les Ultramarines suivent l'organisation structurelle dictée par le Codex Astartes. Cette Tactical Squad a des bords d'épaulière dorés indiquant qu'elle appartient à la 2e Compagnie.

Die Ultramarines folgen der Organisationsstruktur des Codex Astartes exakt. Dieses Tactical Squad hat Schulterpanzer mit Goldrand, der zeigt, dass es der 2. Company angehört.

The Ultramarines believe you must know the enemy before you can fight it. They often use Scout Squads to scope out the enemy forces before battle commences.

Les Ultramarines sont convaincus qu'il faut connaître l'ennemi avant de l'affronter. Ils emploient souvent des Scout Squads pour sonder les forces ennemies avant la bataille.

Die Ultramarines glauben, dass man den Feind kennen muss, bevor man ihn bekämpft. Sie setzten Scout Squads ein, um den Feind vorab auszukundschaften.

The Venerable Dreadnought above bears the names of a dozen worlds in the Ultramar system, worlds it has fought to protect over countless centuries.

Ce Venerable Dreadnought porte les noms d'une douzaine de mondes du système d'Ultramar, ceux pour la protection desquels il a lutté depuis des siècles.

Der Venerable Dreadnought oben trägt den Namen eines Dutzends Welten im Ultramar-System, die er im Laufe unzähliger Jahrhunderte verteidigte.

'EAVY METAL

This month, the 'Eavy Metal team focus their attention on contrasts.

Ce mois-ci, l'équipe 'Eavy Metal porte la plus grande attention aux contrastes.

Diesen Monat konzentriert sich das 'Eavy-Metal-Team auf Kontraste.

There are many contrasts when it comes to painting: light and dark, clean and dirty, hot and cold; the list goes on. The Tyranids on this page are a great example of contrast, light and dark colours placed next to each other to create a striking paint-job.

Il y a plusieurs types de contrastes : clair et obscur, propre et sale, chaud et froid ; et la liste s'allonge. Les tyranids de cette page sont un bel exemple de contrastes, des couleurs claires et sombres juxtaposées pour un résultat saisissant.

Beim Malen gibt es viele Kontraste: hell und dunkel, sauber und schmutzig, warm und kalt; die Liste geht weiter. Die Tyraniden auf dieser Seite sind ein gutes Beispiel für Kontrast. Helle und dunkle Farben nebeneinander erschaffen eine auffallende Bemalung.

This Dark Reaper wears glossy black armour but his weapons and helmet plume are an azure blue, drawing your attention to them. The aspect warrior's bone-coloured helmet is a great example of a strong contrast between light and dark colours.

Ce Dark Reaper porte une armure noir luisant mais son arme et le plumet de son heaume sont d'un bleu azur, qui attire l'attention. Le heaume couleur os de ce guerrier Aspect est un bon exemple de contraste entre couleurs sombres et couleurs claires.

Dieser Dark Reaper trägt glänzend schwarze Rüstung, aber seine Waffen und der Helmbusch sind azurblau und ziehen den Blick an. Der knochenfarbige Helm des Aspect Warriors ist ein gutes Beispiel für einen starken Hell-Dunkel-Kontrast.

This Fire Dragon, on the other hand, has had the colour roles reversed. The model is predominantly bright, with areas such as the weapons and face (the focal parts of the model) picked out black, which has then been highlighted with a contrasting blue.

À l'opposé, les rôles des couleurs sont inversés sur ce Fire Dragon. La figurine est à dominance claire, avec des zones comme les armes et la plaque faciale (éléments importants de la figurine) en noir, qui ont ensuite été éclaircies avec un bleu contrastant.

Die Farbrollen dieses Fire Dragons sind hingegen umgekehrt. Das Modell ist vorwiegend hell und Bereiche wie die Waffen und das Gesicht (die Blickpunkte) wurden schwarz hervorgehoben, welches kontrastreich blau akzentuiert wurde.

READERS' MODELS

The very best of the miniatures photos sent to us by our readers.

Les plus belles photos de figurines peintes envoyées par nos lecteurs.

Die schönsten Miniaturen-bilder, die uns unsere Leser zugeschickt haben.

Khemrian Warsphinx
by Mat Eveleigh.

Stormcast Eternal Liberator
by Oliver Gommer.

Stormcast Eternal Liberator
by Will Vale.

Ultramarines Venerable Dreadnought
by David Colwell.

Imperial Fists Chaplain
by Ryogo Yamane.

Imperial Fists Predator
by Ryogo Yamane.

Putrid Blightking
by John Margiotta.

Blood Angels Librarian
by John Margiotta.

Taur'ruk and Bull Centaur Renders
by Ching Hsiu Hung.

Culexus Assassin
by John Margiotta.

Vindicare Assassin
by John Margiotta.

Infernus, Leman Russ Command Tank
by João David.

Imperial Knight of House Terryn
by Tomasz Przewiezlikowski.

Blood Angels Death Company
by Phil Chang.

Stormcast Eternal Liberator
by Thilo Engels.

Blood Angels Legion Centurion
by Phil Chang.

Skitarii Ranger Alpha
by Gabriele Renna.

Skarbrand the Bloodthirster
by Tomasz Przewiezlikowski.

Want to see your miniatures featured in Readers Models? Send your pictures to:
team@whitedwarf.co.uk

Vous voulez voir votre figurine dans Les Figurines des Lecteurs ? Envoyez vos photos à :
team@whitedwarf.co.uk

Möchtest du deine Miniaturen in dieser Rubrik sehen? Schicke uns deine Bilder an:
team@whitedwarf.co.uk

PARADE GROUND

We present a colourful gallery of miniatures for Warhammer 40,000.

Voici une galerie de figurines hautes en couleurs pour Warhammer 40,000.

Wir präsentieren eine bunte Miniaturengalerie für Warhammer 40,000.

Tech-Priest Dominus, painted by Tom Moore.

Tech-Priest Dominus, peint par Tom Moore.

Tech-Priest Dominus, bemalt von Tom Moore.

This Tyranid Broodlord was painted by Adam Troke. He used a blue and purple scheme on his model to match the classic Space Hulk colour scheme.

Ce Broodlord tyranid a été peint par Adam Troke, qui a employé du bleu et du violet pour correspondre au schéma de couleurs classique de Space Hulk.

Dieser Symbiarch der Tyraniden wurde von Adam Troke bemalt. Er malte ein blau-violettes Schema, das zum klassischen Space-Hulk-Farbschema passt.

Forge World Ryza Kataphron Breachers, painted by Jim Gallagher.

Kataphron Breachers du monde-forge Ryza, peints par Jim Gallagher.

Kataphron Breachers der Fabrikwelt Ryza, bemalt von Jim Gallagher.

Because there is so much silver metal on the Kataphron Breachers, Jim used Leadbelcher spray to basecoat them for quick, effective results. He then painted the armour plates with Jokaero Orange and layered them with Troll Slayer Orange.

Les Kataphron Breachers étant principalement en métal argenté, Jim a utilisé une bombe de Leadbelcher pour les sous-coucher avec un résultat rapide et efficace. Il a ensuite peint l'armure en Jokaero Orange, avant de la dégrader en Troll Slayer Orange.

Da an den Kataphron Breachers so viel silbernes Metall ist, nahm Jim Leadbelcher Spray für schnelle, wirkungsvolle Ergebnisse. Er bemalte dann die Panzerplatten mit Jokaero Orange und schichtete sie mit Troll Slayer Orange.

Blood Angels Drop Pod
by Steve Bowerman.

Drop Pod Blood Angels
par Steve Bowerman.

Blood Angels Drop Pod
von Steve Bowerman.

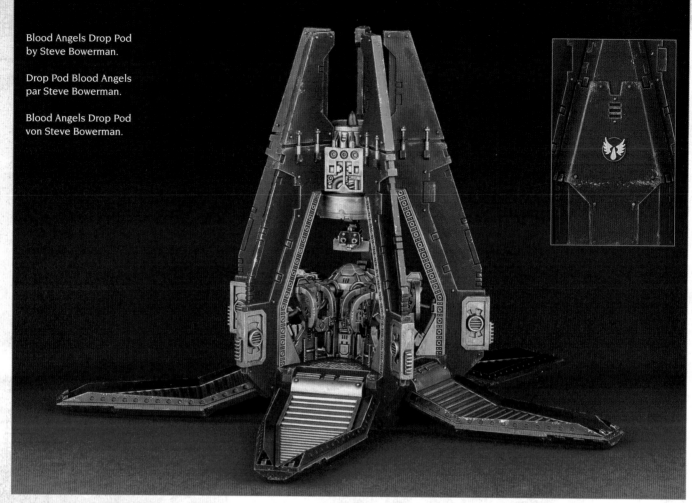

Steve Bowerman also painted this Devastator Squad – note the exemplary attention to detail with correct knee markings and blue Devastator helmets.

Steve Bowerman a également peint cette Devastator Squad. Notez le soin apporté aux détails avec le marquage de genouillère correct et les casques Devastator bleus.

Steve Bowerman bemalte auch dieses Devastator Squad – beachte die Aufmerksamkeit, die er den Kniemarkierungen und blauen Devastator-Helmen widmete.

Steve made his Assault Squad to fight on foot, focussing on dynamic action poses so they all look like they are sprinting forwards into the fight.

Steve a assemblé cette Assault Squad à pied, en se concentrant sur les postures dynamiques de sorte à ce que ces Blood Angels semblent courir droit en mêlée.

Steve lässt sein Assault Squad zu Fuß kämpfen und konzentrierte sich auf dynamische Action-Posen, die aussehen, als sprinte es in den Kampf.

Steve Bowerman's Blood Angels Terminators are from the Space Hulk game. Bearing all the Chapter markings and icons, they're perfect for his burgeoning Blood Angels army.

Les Terminators Blood Angels de Steve Bowerman proviennent du jeu Space Hulk. Tous ornés d'icônes et de marquages du chapitre, ils sont parfaits pour son armée naissante.

Steve Bowermans Blood Angels Terminators stammen aus Space Hulk. Mit all den Markierungen und Symbolen sind sie ideal für seine wachsende Blood-Angels-Armee.

Steve has painted the helmets bone-white. While this departs from the Codex Astartes, he likes how it makes them stand out from their brothers.

Steve a peint les casques en blanc os. Bien que cela diverge du Codex Astartes, il aime voir combien ça les fait ressortir au milieu de leurs frères de bataille.

Steve bemalte die Helme knochenweiß. Auch wenn dies nicht dem Codex Astartes folgt, mag er, wie sie sich dadurch von ihren Brüdern abheben.

Dark Eldar Scourges, painted by Andy Horsfall. They wear the white and black of the Kabal of the Severed Soul.

Scourges Dark Eldar, peints par Andy Horsfall. Ils portent le blanc et le noir de la Kabale de l'Âme Arrachée.

Dark Eldar Scourges, bemalt von Andy Horsfall. Sie tragen das Weiß und Schwarz der Kabale der Verlorenen Seele.

The vivid blue of the Scourges' feathers is Kantor Blue drybrushed with Hoeth Blue and washed with Guilliman Blue.

Le bleu vif des plumes des Scourges est en Kantor Blue brossé à sec en Hoeth Blue suivi d'un lavis de Guilliman Blue.

Das kräftige Blau der Scourge-Federn ist Kantor Blue, trockengebürstet mit Hoeth Blue und getuscht mit Guilliman Blue.

Dark Angels Ravenwing Command Squad, painted by Chris Bilewicz. Chris has used green armour plates and helmets on these Black Knights, a campaign mark across all of his Ravenwing.

Command Squad Ravenwing Dark Angel, peinte par Chris Bilewicz. Chris a ajouté des casques et des plaques vertes à ses Black Knights, une marque de campagne répandue sur sa Ravenwing.

Dark Angels Ravenwing Command Squad, bemalt von Chris Bilewicz. Chris malte bei den Black Knights grüne Schulterpanzer und Helme, Feldzugszeichen seines Ravenwing.

XV95 Ghostkeel, painted by Andy Keddie. Andy's Ghostkeel is named Shas'vre Kesor, a veteran warrior of N'dras Sept.

XV95 Ghostkeel, peinte par Andy Keddie. La Ghostkeel d'Andy est appelée Shas'vre Kesor, un vétéran du sept de N'dras.

XV95 Ghostkeel, bemalt von Andy Keddie. Andys Ghostkeel heißt Shas'vre Kesor, ein Veteranenkrieger der Sept N'dras.

Blood Angels Chaplain by Steve Bowerman. Steve has used certain colours to unify elements of his army. Note the blood drop gem and the purple handle of the crozius arcanum, which match similar details on his other Blood Angels.

Chaplain Blood Angel par Steve Bowerman. Steve a utilisé certaines couleurs pour unifier les éléments de son armée. Notez la gemme de sang et le manche violet de son crozius, qui font écho aux détails de ses autres Blood Angels.

Blood Angels Chaplain von Steve Bowerman. Steve verwendete bestimmte Farben, zur Vereinigung seiner Armee. Beachte den Blutstropfenstein und den Griff des Crozius Arcanums, die Details an seinen anderen Blood Angels ähneln.

House Drakkus Imperial
Knight Warden, painted by
Paul Norton.

Imperial Knight Warden
de la maison Drakkus,
peint par Paul Norton.

House Drakkus Imperial
Knight Warden, bemalt von
Paul Norton.

Paul painted this Imperial
Knight in the colours of
House Drakkus, the
household featured in the
videogame Warhammer
40,000: Freeblade.

Paul a peint cet Imperial
Knight aux couleurs de la
maison Drakkus, celle mise
à l'honneur dans le jeu
vidéo Warhammer 40,000:
Freeblade.

Paul bemalte diesen
Imperial Knight in den
Farben von House Drakkus,
dem Hausverband im
Videospiel „Warhammer
40,000: Freeblade".

Paul applied extensive, but subtle, weathering to the armour plates of this Knight, with scores of tiny scratches picked out with Citadel Edge paints. Rhinox Hide details make some scratches look so deep they've bared metal.

Paul a appliqué une usure généralisée mais subtile aux plaques de son Knight, avec des micro-éraflures peintes en Citadel Edge. Des détails en Rhinox Hide ajoutent de la profondeur à certaines éraflures comme si le métal avait été mis à nu.

Paul alterte die Panzerung dieses Knights ausgiebig aber subtil mit vielen winzigen Kratzern, die mit Citadel-Edge-Farben hervorgehoben wurden. Durch Rhinox Hide sehen einige Kratzer aus, als gingen sie tief ins Metall.

House Drakkus is an Imperial-aligned house, famed for fighting against Chaos, especially the warriors of Khorne. In the game Freeblade, you fight to avenge the brothers of your household slain in a brutal ambush.

La maison Drakkus, affiliée à l'Imperium, est célèbre pour affronter le Chaos, surtout les guerriers de Khorne. Dans le jeu Freeblade, vous luttez pour venger les frères de votre maison fauchés lors d'une brutale embuscade.

House Drakkus ist ein imperiumstreues House, bekannt für Kämpfe gegen das Chaos, besonders die Krieger Khornes. Im Spiel Freeblade rächst du die Brüder deines Hausverbands, die in einem brutalen Hinterhalt fielen.

House Drakkus Imperial Knight Paladin, painted by Natalie Slinn.

Imperial Knight Paladin de la maison Drakkus, peint par Natalie Slinn.

House Drakkus Imperial Knight Paladin, bemalt von Natalie Slinn.

Natalie has painted this Imperial Knight suit with a single carapace stripe to show that the pilot holds the rank of Baron, making him head of his household.

Natalie a peint cet Imperial Knight avec une seule bande pour montrer que son pilote tient le rang de baron, ce qui le place à la tête de sa maison.

Natalie bemalte diesen Knight mit einem Streifen auf der Rückenpanzerung als Zeichen, dass der Pilot ein Baron ist, Oberhaupt des Hausverbands.

The House Drakkus heraldry (both the house crest and the shoulder emblem) on this Knight, as well as those on Paul's on the previous page, are taken from a special decal sheet released to celebrate the Freeblade game.

L'héraldique de la maison Drakkus (à la fois sur ses armoiries et son emblème d'épaule) sur ce Knight, ainsi que sur celui de Paul page précédente, provient d'une planche de décalcomanies sortie en l'honneur du jeu Freeblade.

Die Heraldik von House Drakkus (sowohl Wappen als auch Schulteremblem) auf diesem Knight, ebenso auf Pauls auf der vorherigen Seite, sind von einem Abziehbilderbogen zur Feier des Erscheinens des Freeblade-Spiels.

The exoskeleton of Natalie's Knight suit is nice and clean (the sacristans have clearly worked hard on the Baron's armour). It was painted with Leadbelcher washed with Nuln Oil and drybrushed with Necron Compound.

L'exosquelette du Knight de Natalie est rutilant, (à l'évidence, les sacristans ont travaillé dur sur l'armure du baron). Il a été peint en Leadbelcher, avant de recevoir un lavis de Nuln Oil, puis un brossage à sec de Necron Compound.

Das Exoskelett von Natalies Knight ist schön sauber (die Sakristane haben hart an der Rüstung des Barons gearbeitet). Es wurde mit Leadbelcher bemalt, mit Nuln Oil getuscht und mit Necron Compound gebürstet.

AERIS AESTUS

A collection of Imperial Knights by Magos Dominus Tom Harrison.

Une collection d'Imperial Knights par le Magos Dominus Tom Harrison.

Die Imperial-Knights-Sammlung von Magos Dominus Tom Harrison.

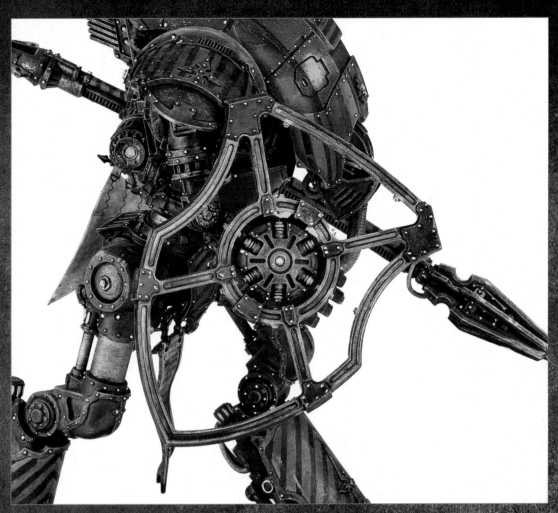

Tom's Imperial Knights are from an unknown household, the rusted relics of a bygone age. Recovered by Magos Dominus Infirmum Octo, they now fight for the Omnissiah once more.

Les Imperial Knights de Tom sont issus d'une maison inconnue, les reliques rouillées d'un âge passé. Retrouvés par le Magos Dominus Infirmum Octo, ils luttent à nouveau pour l'Omnimessie.

Toms Imperial Knights entstammen einem unbekannten House. Sie sind verrostete Relikte früherer Zeiten, die dank Magos Dominus Infirmum Octo nun erneut für den Omnissiah kämpfen.

Magos Infirmum Octo is widely regarded by his peers as a radical for hunting down forbidden technology. It's rumoured that this Knight Lancer, *Aurora Column*, is the fruit of his labours.

Le Magos Infirmum Octo est considéré par ses pairs comme radical pour sa quête des technologies interdites. On raconte que ce Knight Lancer, *Aurora Column*, est le fruit de ses laborieux travaux.

Magos Infirmum Octo ist unter Seinesgleichen als radikaler Jäger verbotener Technologien bekannt. Es heißt, dass dieser Knight Lancer, *Aurora Column*, Frucht seiner Bemühungen sei.

Tempestas Cantor, Imperial
Knight Warden.

Tempestas Cantor, Imperial
Knight Warden.

Tempestas Cantor, Imperial
Knight Warden.

Tom's Knights are painted
to look old and rusty, as if
they've been in storage for
millennia. It's rumoured
their pilots are grafted into
their Knight suits.

Les Knights de Tom sont
peints vieux et rouillés,
comme ayant été remisés
durant des millénaires.
Leurs pilotes seraient
greffés à leurs Knights.

Toms Knights sind so
bemalt, dass sie alt und
rostig wirken, als seien sie
ewig nicht benutzt worden.
Man munkelt, die Piloten
seien in ihnen eingelassen.

Quantum Lux, Imperial
Knight Crusader.

Quantum Lux, Imperial
Knight Crusader.

Quantum Lux, Imperial
Knight Crusader.

Tom converted *Quantum Lux* using a light and wall panel from the Basilica Administratum for the head and tilting shield respectively.

Tom a converti *Quantum Lux* à l'aide d'un projecteur et d'une cloison du kit de Basilica Administratum pour la tête et l'écu respectivement.

Tom baute *Quantum Lux* mit einer Lampe und einem Mauerstück der Basilica Administratum um, um Kopf und Wappenschild damit zu ersetzen.

Fulminis Iactum, Questoris
Knight Magaera.

Fulminis Iactum, Questoris
Knight Magaera.

Fulminis Iactum, Questoris
Knight Magaera.

Tom was inspired to paint
these Knights after seeing
some of John Blanche's
illustrations. The dirty,
gritty style is certainly
reminiscent of John's work.

Tom a été inspiré pour
peindre ces Knights après
avoir vu des illustrations de
John Blanche. Le style sale,
et graveleux rappelant
assurément l'œuvre de John.

Tom wurde bei diesen
Knights von John Blanches
Illustrationen inspiriert.
Der schmutzige, bizarre Stil
ist sehr typisch für Johns
Arbeiten.

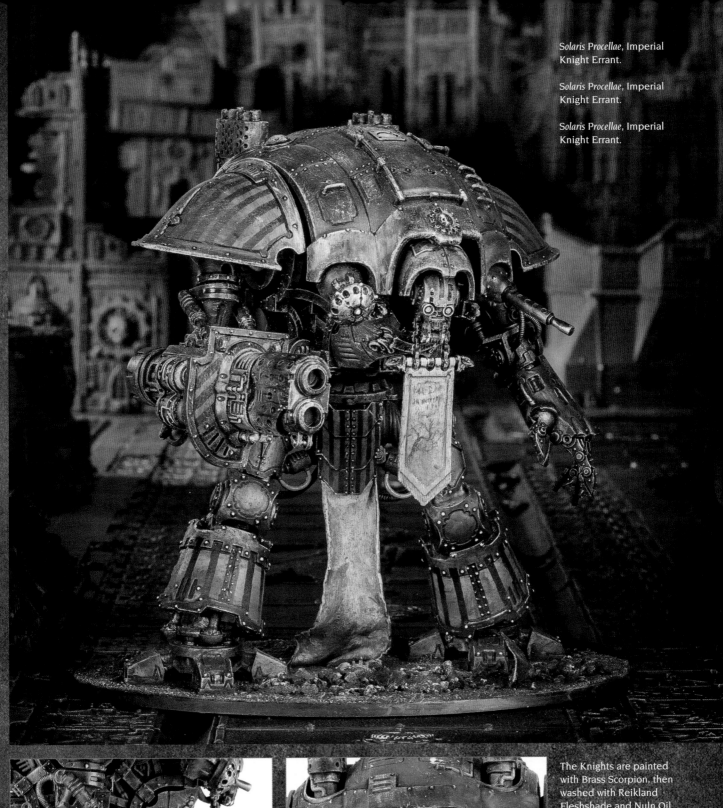

Solaris Procellae, Imperial Knight Errant.

Solaris Procellae, Imperial Knight Errant.

Solaris Procellae, Imperial Knight Errant.

The Knights are painted with Brass Scorpion, then washed with Reikland Fleshshade and Nuln Oil before being covered in weathering powders.

Les Knights sont peints en Brass Scorpion, puis reçoivent un lavis de Reikland Fleshshade et de Nuln Oil avant d'être couverts de pigments.

Die Knights sind mit Brass Scorpion bemalt, dann mit Reikland Fleshshade und Nuln Oil getuscht, ehe sie mit Weathering Powders bedeckt wurden.

Aes Domino, the Brass Lord, Warhound Titan of Legio Aeris Aestus and champion of Magos Octo's warband.

Aes Domino, le Seigneur d'Airain, Titan Warhound de la Legio Aeris Aestus et champion de la bande du Magos Octo.

Aes Domino, der Messingfürst, Warhound Titan der Legio Aeris Aestus und Champion von Magos Octos Streitmacht.

The Warhound was painted the same way as Tom's Knights, but with a pale bone-coloured carapace to make it stand out. The scribblings and diagrams across the carapace were drawn on using a pencil, then darkened using illustrating inks.

Le Warhound a été peint de la même façon que les Knights de Tom, mais avec une carapace couleur os pour le distinguer. Les inscriptions et les diagrammes sur la carapace ont été tracés au crayon, puis, assombris avec des encres pour illustration.

Der Warhound wurde genauso bemalt wie Toms Knights, jedoch mit einem knochenfarbenen Rumpf, um ihn abzuheben. Die Beschriftungen und Diagramme wurden mit dem Bleistift aufgetragen und dann mit Illustratoren-Tinte abgedunkelt.

We present a gallery of Space Marines from the Horus Heresy. First up, a unit of Salamanders painted by Chris Webb.

Voici une galerie de space marines de l'Hérésie d'Horus. Tout d'abord, une unité de Salamanders peinte par Chris Webb.

Wir präsenieren eine Galerie mit Space Marines aus der Horus-Häresie. Zuerst eine Einheit Salamanders von Chris Webb.

Iron Warriors by Ian Strickland – like all the squads here, made using plastic Space Marines from the Betrayal at Calth set.

Iron Warriors par Ian Strickland – comme toutes les escouades ici, assemblés avec les Space Marines de Betrayal at Calth.

Iron Warriors von Ian Strickland – wie alle Squads hier aus Kunststoff-Space-Marines aus dem „Betrayal at Calth"-Set gebaut.

Like all the models in this gallery, these White Scars by Neil Cook were converted using Forge World upgrade packs.

Comme toutes les figurines de cette galerie, ces White Scars par Neil Cook ont été convertis avec des packs Forge World.

Wie alle Modelle in dieser Galerie wurden diese White Scars (von Neil Cook) mit Upgrade Packs von Forge World umgebaut.

These Night Lords legionaries, painted by Gary Shaw, have freehand lightning bolts painted on to their armour.

Ces légionnaires Night Lords, peints par Gary Shaw, ont des éclairs peints à main levée sur leurs armures.

Diese Legionäre der Night Lords, bemalt von Gary Shaw, bekamen freihändig Blitze auf ihrer Rüstung aufgemalt.

Jamie Forster painted these Raven Guard legionaries, each model converted with parts from the Raven Guard upgrade pack.

Jamie Forster a peint ces légionnaires Raven Guard, tous convertis avec des éléments du pack d'amélioration Raven Guard.

Jamie Forster bemalte diese Raven Guard Legionaries. Jedes Modell wurde mit dem Raven Guard Upgrade Pack umgebaut.

This unit of Death Guard painted by Paul Rudge feature transfers available from the Forge World website.

Cette unité de Death Guard peinte par Paul Rudge utilise des décaclomanies disponibles sur le site Web de Forge World.

Die Abziehbilder dieser Death-Guard-Einheit von Paul Rudge sind auf der Website von Forge World erhältlich.

The once-white armour of James Karch's World Eaters is caked in the blood, mud and filth of the battlefield.

Les armures jadis blanches des World Eaters de James Karch sont maculées de sang, de boue et de la crasse du champ de bataille.

Die einst weiße Rüstung von James Karchs World Eaters ist mit Blut, Matsch und dem Schmutz des Schlachtfelds verkrustet.

Rob McFarlane's Iron Hands wear older Mk. III Iron armour helmets to show their veteran status within the Legion.

Les Iron Hands de Rob McFarlane portent des casques Mk. III Iron pour montrer leur statut de vétérans au sein de la légion.

Rob McFarlanes Iron Hands tragen Helme der älteren Typ-III-Eisen-Rüstung, die zeigen, dass sie Legions-Veteranen sind.

These Word Bearers were painted by Dominik Oedinger, who gave them a dirty, battle-worn appearance.

These Word Bearers were painted by Dominik Oedinger, who gave them a dirty, battle-worn appearance.

These Word Bearers were painted by Dominik Oedinger, who gave them a dirty, battle-worn appearance.

This Sons of Horus squad by John Bell was airbrushed using the Forge World airbrush paint Sons of Horus Green.

This Sons of Horus squad by John Bell was airbrushed using the Forge World airbrush paint Sons of Horus Green.

This Sons of Horus squad by John Bell was airbrushed using the Forge World airbrush paint Sons of Horus Green.

These Imperial Fists, painted by Owen Patten, wear campaign markings (Forge World decals) from the Great Crusade.

These Imperial Fists, painted by Owen Patten, wear campaign markings (Forge World decals) from the Great Crusade.

These Imperial Fists, painted by Owen Patten, wear campaign markings (Forge World decals) from the Great Crusade.

Andy Hoare's Emperor's Children were painted silver, then airbrushed with the new Eidolon Purple clear paint.

Andy Hoare's Emperor's Children were painted silver, then airbrushed with the new Eidolon Purple clear paint.

Andy Hoare's Emperor's Children were painted silver, then airbrushed with the new Eidolon Purple clear paint.

PARADE GROUND

We present a gallery of models painted for Warhammer Age of Sigmar.

Voici une galerie de figurines peintes pour Warhammer Age of Sigmar.

Eine Galerie mit Modellen, die für Warhammer Age of Sigmar bemalt wurden.

Bloodthirster of Unfettered Fury, painted by Stuart Black. Check out the fantastic effect that makes the Bloodthirster appear to be walking on flames.

Bloodthirster of Unfettered Fury, peint par Stuart Black. Observez le fantastique effet donnant l'impression que le Bloodthirster marche sur des flammes.

Bloodthirster of Unfettered Fury von Stuart Black. Beachte den tollen Effekt, der es wirken lässt als wandle der Bloodthirster auf Flammen.

Khorne Bloodletters by Stuart Black. Stuart has used Citadel Dry paints and Shades for the ruddy skin tone on these (and also the Bloodthirster opposite).

Khorne Bloodletters par Stuart Black. Stuart a utilisé des peintures Citadel Dry et des Shade pour obtenir ce ton de peau rougeâtre (ainsi que sur le Bloodthirster ci-contre).

Khorne Bloodletters von Stuart Black. Stuart verwendete Citadel-Dry-Farben und Shades für die rote Haut dieser Modelle (und des Bloodthirsters gegenüber).

The bases on Stuart's models were done using Martian Ironearth, giving them the appearance of tortured and cracked ground, perfect for the Mortal Realms.

Les socles des figurines de Stuart ont été réalisés en Martian Ironearth, qui donne l'apparence d'un sol torturé et craquelé, idéal pour les Royaumes Mortels.

Stuart bemalte die Bases mit Martian Ironearth und ließ sie aufgeplatzt und aufgerissen aussehen, perfekt für die Reiche der Sterblichen.

Khorne Blood Warriors, painted by Stuart Black. The bloodstained blades were painted with lashings of Blood for the Blood God Technical paint.

Khorne Blood Warriors, peints par Stuart Black. Les lames tachées de sang ont été peintes avec des projections de peinture Technical Blood for the Blood God.

Blood Warriors des Khorne von Stuart Black. Die blutigen Klingen bemalte er mit Spritzern der Technical-Farbe Blood for the Blood God.

Chaos Chosen by Steve Bowerman. Steve has painted their armour plates green, in homage to the Plague God Nurgle.

Chaos Chosen par Steve Bowerman. Steve a peint les plates d'armure en vert en hommage à Nurgle, le Dieu des Pestes.

Chaos Chosen von Steve Bowerman. Er bemalte die Panzerplatten grün, um den Seuchengott Nurgle zu ehren.

These Nurgle warriors have been painted with cold colours, an effect that is finished off with Citadel Snow on their bases.

Ces Guerriers de Nurgle ont été peints en couleurs froides, un effet parachevé en ajoutant de la Neige Citadel sur leurs socles.

Diese Krieger des Nurgle wurden mit kalten Farben bemalt und der Effekt mit Citadel-Schnee auf den Bases vollendet.

Gaunt Summoner of Tzeentch by Jes Bickham. This enslaved servant of Archaon is the glue that binds the disparate elements of Jes's Chaos army together, ensuring all his warriors willingly serve the Everchosen.

Gaunt Summoner de Tzeentch par Jes Bickham. Ce serviteur asservi par Archaon est la glu qui lie les éléments disparates de l'armée du Chaos de Jes, veillant à ce que tous ses guerriers servent de bon gré l'Élu Éternel.

Gaunt Summoner des Tzeentch von Jes Bickham. Dieser Diener Archaons verbindet die einzelnen Elemente von Jes' Chaosarmee und stellt sicher, dass alle darin bereitwillig dem Ewig Auserwählten dienen.

Khorgorath by Jes Bickham. Jes has painted this warp-twisted monster with disturbing fleshy tones, emphasising its origins as a brutish creature mutated by the power of Chaos. It's even more horrific like this than the traditional red.

Khorgorath par Jes Bickham. Jes a peint ce monstre corrompu en tons de chair perturbant, accentuant ses origines de créature brutale mutée par le pouvoir du Chaos. Il en est même plus horrible que la version rouge traditionnelle.

Khorgorath von Jes Bickham. Er bemalte dieses warpverzerrte Monster in verstörend fleischigen Farben, was seinen Ursprung als chaosmutierte Kreatur betont. So ist er noch schrecklicher als im traditionellen Rot.

Krell, Mortarch of Despair and a regiment of Skeleton Warriors, painted by James Littler. Krell advances over a mound of bones and skeletal remains. We love the ghostly green glow James used on his models, especially how it emanates from the gaps in Krell's plate armour.

Krell, Mortarch of Despair et régiment de Skeleton Warriors, peints par James Littler. Krell avance sur un monceau d'ossements. Nous adorons la lueur fantomatique qui James a employé sur ses figurines, surtout la façon dont elle émane des fentes entre les plates d'armure de Krell.

Krell, der Mortarch of Despair, und ein Regiment Skeleton Warriors von James Littler. Krell marschiert über einen Haufen Skelettüberreste. Wir lieben das geisterhaft grüne Leuchten auf James' Modellen, besonders die Art wie es aus den Lücken in Krells Rüstung dringt.

These Nighthaunt Spirit Hosts were also painted by James – note how he has added spare bits and even Skeleton Warriors to detail their bases.

Ces Nighthaunt Spirit Hosts ont également été peintes par James – notez comment il a ajouté des pièces et même des Skeleton Warriors pour détailler ses socles.

Auch diese Nighthaunt Spirits hat James bemalt – beachte, wie er übrige Teile und sogar Skeleton Warriors verwendete, um die Bases zu gestalten.

The eerie green glow on the Skeletons was done by applying a Waywatcher Green glaze over Corax White undercoat, then drybrushing it with Praxeti White.

La lueur verte sur les Skeletons a été obtenue avec un glacis de Waywatcher Green sur une sous-couche de Corax White, avant de brosser à sec en Praxeti White.

Das grüne Leuchten der Skeletons erzeugte er mit Waywatcher Green auf einer Grundierung mit Corax White und Trockenbürsten mit Praxeti White.

Lord of Plagues and Putrid Blightkings, painted by Pete Foley. These are the first models in Pete's new Rotbringers army. We're hoping he does lots more.

Lord of Plagues et Putrid Blightkings peints par Pete Foley, les premières figurines de sa nouvelle armée de Rotbringers. Nous espérons qu'il en peindra plein d'autres.

Lord of Plagues und Putrid Blightkings von Pete Foley. Dies sind die ersten Modelle seiner neuen Rotbringers-Armee. Wir hoffen, dass noch viele folgen werden.

Pete has contrasted dark green armour plates with the pallid flesh of his Blightkings. Blood for the Blood God glistens in all the gaping wounds.

Pete a contrasté des plaques d'armure verte avec la chair pâle de ses Blightkings. Du Blood for the Blood God luit dans toutes les plaies béantes.

Pete erzeugt einen Kontrast zwischen dunkelgrüner Rüstung und blassem Fleisch der Blightkings. In den Wunden schimmert Blood for the Blood God.

The sonorous tocsin and Chaos icons borne by these Blightkings are stained with verdigris (Nihilakh Oxide) and weep pus (Nurgle's Rot) from the pockmarks.

Le tocsin et les icônes du Chaos portés par ces Blightkings sont constellés de vert-de-gris (Nihilakh Oxide) et suintent du pus (Nurgle's Rot) de leurs entailles.

Die Sonore Glocke und die Chaosikone dieser Blightkings sind mit Grünspan (Nihilakh Oxide) und triefendem Eiter (Nurgle's Rot) aus den Pocken befleckt.

Superbly applied shading captures every last sagging fold, moist wrinkle and torn chunk of ragged flesh on these Blightkings. We especially love (and yet are also repulsed by) the raw exposed flesh seen in the skin-tears.

Des ombres superbement appliquées capturent chaque repli, bourrelets juteux et lambeaux de chair de ces Blightkings. Nous adorons (et sommes tous autant révulsés par) la chair à vif visible dans les trous de la peau.

Hervorragende Schattierungen heben jede Fleischschicht, feuchte Falte und herausgerissenen Fleischfetzen hervor. Besonders gefällt uns (auch wenn es uns gleichzeitig anwidert) das freigelegte Fleisch in den Hautrissen.

Grimwrath Berzerker and Hearthguard Berzerkers by Kevin Chin. Kevin has been inspired by the artwork of Grimnir in Battletome: Fyreslayers, with his blazing skin as he battles Vulcatrix. He's used Citadel Shades and Glazes to create the same colours and effects on his models.

Grimwrath Berzerker et Hearthguard Berzerkers par Kevin Chin. Kevin a été inspiré par l'illustration de Grimnir dans le Battletome : Fyreslayers, avec sa peau luisante comme il affronte Vulcatrix. Il a utilisé les Citadel Shade et Glaze pour créer les mêmes effets et teintes sur ses figurines.

Grimwrath Berzerkers und Hearthguard Berzerkers von Kevin Chin. Kevin wurde von Artwork von Grimnir in Battletome: Fyreslayers inspiriert, in dem er mit brennender Haut Vulcatrix bekämpfte. Er benutzte Shades und Glazes, um dieselben Farben und Effekte zu erzeugen.

Khorne Bloodreavers by Chris Peach. Chris has been building up a Bloodbound army over several months – they wear the colours of the Iron Horde.

Khorne Bloodreavers par Chris Peach. Chris a assemblé une armée de Bloodbound ces derniers mois – ils portent les couleurs de l'Iron Horde.

Khorne Bloodreavers von Chris Peach. Er hat im Laufe einiger Monate eine Bloodbound-Armee aufgebaut, die die Farben der Iron Horde trägt.

Chris has made a few subtle conversions on his Bloodreavers – a keen eye can see where he's used heads from other models in the Chaos range.

Chris a effectué des conversions subtiles sur ses Bloodreavers – un œil observateur verra qu'il a utilisé des têtes d'autres figurines de la gamme du Chaos.

Chris hat seine Bloodreavers an ein paar Stellen dezent umgebaut – ein geschultes Auge sieht sofort, welche Köpfe von anderen Modellen des Chaos stammen.

PAINT SPLATTER

Stage-by-stage guides on how to paint the Wulfen and Ulrik the Slayer.

Schritt-für-Schritt-Bemalanleitungen für die Wulfen und Ulrik the Slayer.

Guides de peinture pas-à-pas pour les Wulfen et Ulrik the Slayer.

SPACE WOLVES WULFEN

SKIN

1
Basecoat: Bugman's Glow
S Base

2
Layer: Cadian Fleshtone
M Layer

3
Wash: Reikland Fleshshade
M Glaze

4
Layer: Cadian Fleshtone
M Layer

5
Layer: Kislev Flesh
S Layer

6
Layer: Flayed One Flesh
S Layer

FACIAL DETAILS

1
Basecoat: Blood for the Blood God
XS Artificer Layer

2
Basecoat: Rhinox Hide
S Layer

3
Layer: Ushabti Bone
XS Artificer Layer

BLACK CARAPACE

1
Basecoat: Abaddon Black
S Base

2
Layer: Dark Reaper
S Layer

3
Layer: Administratum Grey
XS Artificer Layer

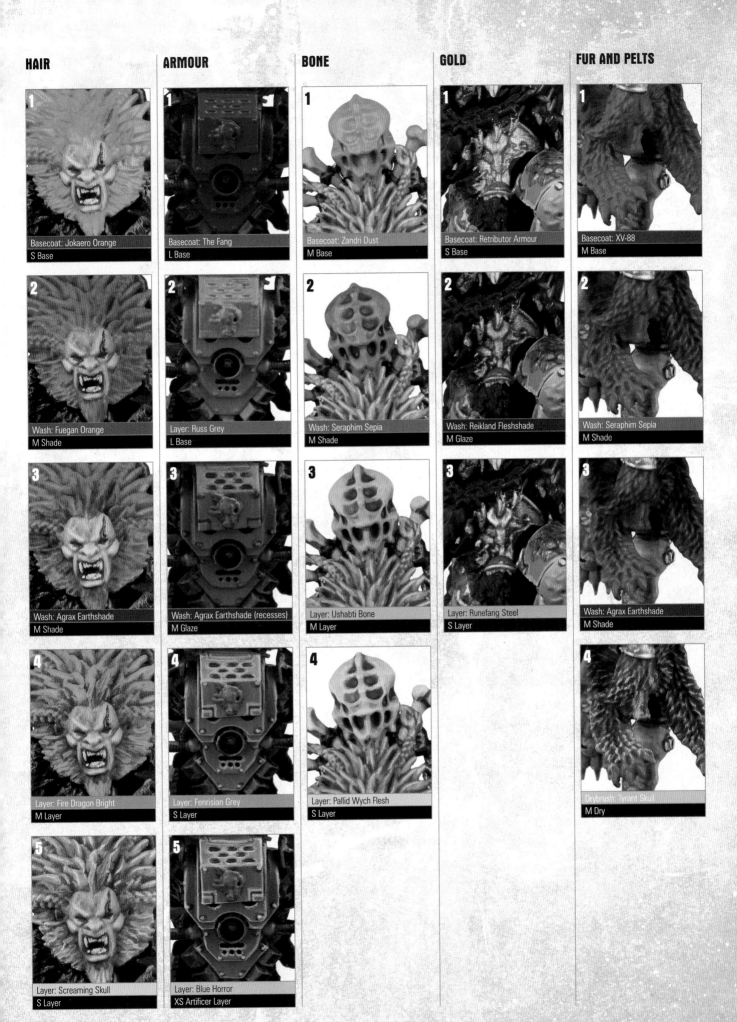

HAIR

1
Basecoat: Jokaero Orange
S Base

2
Wash: Fuegan Orange
M Shade

3
Wash: Agrax Earthshade
M Shade

4
Layer: Fire Dragon Bright
M Layer

5
Layer: Screaming Skull
S Layer

ARMOUR

1
Basecoat: The Fang
L Base

2
Layer: Russ Grey
L Base

3
Wash: Agrax Earthshade (recesses)
M Glaze

4
Layer: Fenrisian Grey
S Layer

5
Layer: Blue Horror
XS Artificer Layer

BONE

1
Basecoat: Zandri Dust
M Base

2
Wash: Seraphim Sepia
M Shade

3
Layer: Ushabti Bone
M Layer

4
Layer: Pallid Wych Flesh
S Layer

GOLD

1
Basecoat: Retributor Armour
S Base

2
Wash: Reikland Fleshshade
M Glaze

3
Layer: Runefang Steel
S Layer

FUR AND PELTS

1
Basecoat: XV-88
M Base

2
Wash: Seraphim Sepia
M Shade

3
Wash: Agrax Earthshade
M Shade

4
Drybrush: Tyrant Skull
M Dry

FROST CLAWS

1

Basecoat: Ceramite White
S Base

2
Glaze: Guilliman Blue
M Glaze

3
Layer: Ulthuan Grey
M Layer

4
Layer: White Scar
S Layer

5
Layer: Runefang Steel
XS Artificer Layer

PACK MARKINGS

1
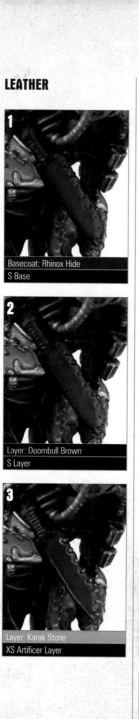
Basecoat: Ceramite White
S Base

2
Layer: Mephiston Red
M Layer

3
Wash: Agrax Earthshade
M Glaze

LEATHER

1
Basecoat: Rhinox Hide
S Base

2
Layer: Doombull Brown
S Layer

3
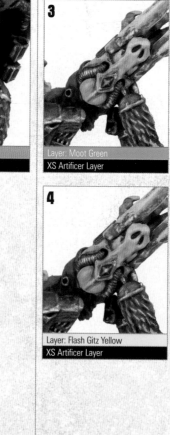
Layer: Karak Stone
XS Artificer Layer

GEMS

1
Basecoat: Caliban Green
M Layer

2
Layer: Warpstone Glow
S Layer

3
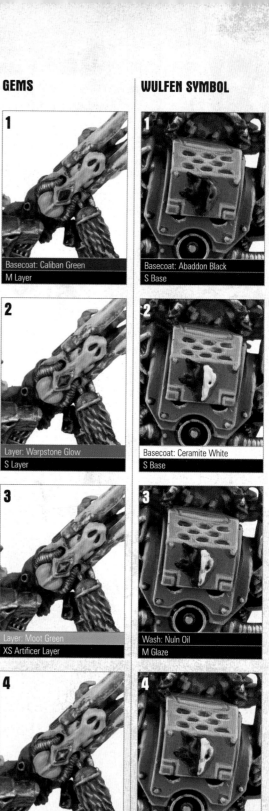
Layer: Moot Green
XS Artificer Layer

4
Layer: Flash Gitz Yellow
XS Artificer Layer

WULFEN SYMBOL

1
Basecoat: Abaddon Black
S Base

2
Basecoat: Ceramite White
S Base

3
Wash: Nuln Oil
M Glaze

4

Layer: Dark Reaper
S Layer

5

Layer: Administratum Grey
XS Artificer Layer

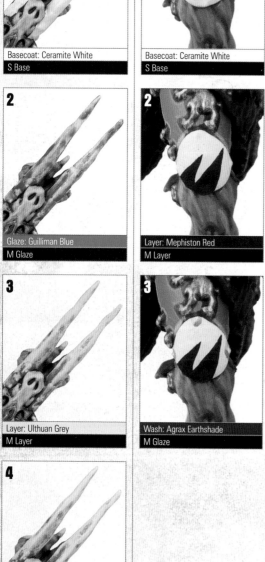

Howling packs of Wulfen hurl themselves into the fray, their appetite for slaughter spreading to the Space Wolves in their wake.

Des meutes de Wulfens hurlants se ruent en mêlée, leur soif de massacre s'étendant aux Space Wolves dans leur sillage.

Heulende Wulfenrudel werfen sich in die Schlacht. Ihr Hunger auf Gemetzel breitet sich auf die Space Wolves hinter ihnen aus.

ULRIK THE SLAYER

BLACK ARMOUR

1
Basecoat: Abaddon Black
L Base

2
Layer: Dark Reaper
M Layer

3
Layer: Fenrisian Grey
S Layer

YELLOW

1
Basecoat: Averland Sunset
S Base

2
Wash: Seraphim Sepia
M Shade

3
Layer: Yriel Yellow
M Layer

4
Layer: Screaming Skull
S Layer

WOLF PELTS

1
Basecoat: Rakarth Flesh
M Base

2
Layer: Ushabti Bone
M Base

3
Wash: Seraphim Sepia
L Shade

4
Wash: Seraphim Sepia (upper part)
M Shade

5
Wash: Agrax Earthshade
M Shade

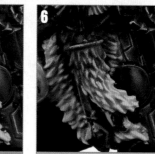
6
Layer: Ushabti Bone
M Layer

7
Layer: Pallid Wych Flesh
S Layer

RED CLOAK

1
Basecoat: Khorne Red
L Base

2
Wash: Nuln Oil
L Shade

3
Layer: Evil Sunz Scarlet
M Layer

4
Layer: Fire Dragon Bright
S Layer

5
Layer: Pallid Wych Flesh
XS Artificer Layer

BONE

1
Basecoat: Zandri Dust
S Base

2
Layer: Ushabti Bone
S Base

3
Wash: Seraphim Sepia
M Shade

4
Layer: Ushabti Bone
M Layer

5
Layer: Screaming Skull
S Layer

6
Layer: White Scar
XS Artificer Layer

FACE AND BEARD

1
Basecoat: Bugman's Glow
S Base

2
Layer: Kislev Flesh
S Base

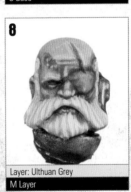

3
Wash: Reikland Fleshshade
M Shade

4
Layer: Kislev Flesh
M Layer

5
Layer: Xereus Purple (scar)
XS Artificer Layer

6
Layer: Flayed One Flesh
XS Artificer Layer

7
Basecoat: Celestra Grey
S Base

8
Layer: Ulthuan Grey
M Layer

9
Layer: White Scar
S Layer

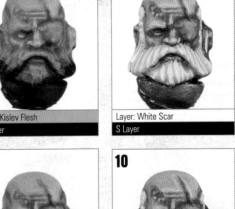

10
Wash: Nuln Oil (recesses)
S Layer

GOLD

1
Basecoat: Retributor Armour
M Base

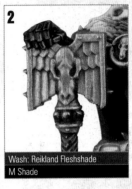

2
Wash: Reikland Fleshshade
M Shade

3
Layer: Auric Armour Gold
M Layer

4
Layer: Runefang Steel
S Layer

STORE FINDER

Games Workshop has its own network of stores worldwide, which stock a wide range of Citadel miniatures, books and other products – here you'll find every one of them listed.

Games Workshop dispose de son propre réseau de magasins à travers le monde, lesquels disposent d'une large gamme de figurines Citadel, de jeux, livres et autres produits. En voici la liste complète.

Games Workshop verfügt über eine eigene Kette von Läden, die weltweit eine große Auswahl an Citadel-Miniaturen, Büchern und anderen Produkten vorrätig haben – hier findest du sie alle.

UK

Games Workshop Aberdeen
12-14 Upper Kirkgate
Aberdeen, AB10 1BA
Tel: 01224 649779
Facebook: GWAberdeen

Warhammer Altrincham
49 Railway Street
Altrincham, WA14 2RQ
Tel: 0161 9299896
Facebook:
WarhammerAltrincham

Games Workshop Ashford
Unit 17, Park Mall Shopping
Centre, Ashford, TN24 8RY
Tel: 01233 632960
Facebook:
GamesWorkshopAshford

Games Workshop Aylesbury
6 Market Street
Aylesbury, HP20 2PN
Tel: 01296 429703
Facebook: GWAylesbury

Games Workshop Ayr
Unit 2 Lorne Arcade
115 High Street, Ayr, KA7 1SB
Tel: 01292 285650
Facebook: GWAyr

Games Workshop Banbury
1a Church Lane
Banbury, OX16 5LR
Tel: 01295 251078
Facebook: GWBanbury

Games Workshop Barnet
7c High Street
Barnet, EN5 5UE
Tel: 0208 2165862
Facebook: GWBarnet

Games Workshop Barnstaple
8 Queens House, Queen Street
Barnstaple, EX32 8HJ
Tel: 01271 859115
Facebook: GWBarnstaple

Games Workshop Basildon
Ground Floor, Axis Development
Southernhay
Basildon, SS14 1LG
Tel: 01268 280192
Facebook: GWBasildon

Games Workshop Basingstoke
3 Potters Walk
Basingstoke, RG21 7GQ
Tel: 01256 466050
Facebook: GWBasingstoke

Warhammer Bath
15 St James Parade
Bath, BA1 1UL
Tel: 01225 334044
Facebook: WarhammerBath

Games Workshop Bedford
10 Greyfriars
Bedford, MK40 1HP
Tel: 01234 273663
Facebook: GWBedford

Games Workshop Belfast
20A Castle Court
Belfast, BT1 1DD
Tel: 02890 233684
Facebook: GWBelfast

Games Workshop Bexleyheath
193 The Broadway
Bexleyheath, Kent, DA6 7ER
Tel: 0208 301 4463
Facebook: GWBexleyheath

Games Workshop Birmingham
36 Priory Queensway
Birmingham, B4 7LA
Tel: 0121 2334840
Facebook: GWBirmingham

Games Workshop Blackpool
8 Birley Street
Blackpool, FY1 1DU
Tel: 01253 752056
Facebook: GWBlackpool

Games Workshop Bolton
Unit 14, The Gates
Crompton Place
Bolton, BL1 1DF
Tel: 01204 362131
Facebook: GWBolton

Games Workshop Boston
45 Wide Bargate, Boston
Lincolnshire, PE21 6SH
Tel: 01205 356596
Facebook: GWBoston

Games Workshop Bournemouth
85 Commercial Road
Bournemouth, BH2 5RT
Tel: 01202 319292
Facebook: GWBournemouth

Games Workshop Bradford
4 Picadilly
Bradford, BD1 3LW
Tel: 01274 739430
Facebook: GWBradford

Games Workshop Brentwood
Unit 39, Ongar Road
Brentwood, CM15 9AU
Tel: 01277 230645
Facebook: GWBrentwood

Games Workshop Brighton
Unit 7, Nile Pavilions
Nile Street
Brighton, BN1 1HW
Tel: 01273 203333
Facebook: GWBrighton

Games Workshop Bristol
33b Wine Street
Bristol, BS1 2BQ
Tel: 0117 9251533
Facebook: GWBristol

Games Workshop Bromley
Unit 24, The Mall
Bromley, BR1 1TS
Tel: 0208 4660678
Facebook: GWBromley

Games Workshop Burton
Unit B, Union Court
Union Street, Burton-upon-Trent
Staffordshire, DE14 1AA
Tel: 01283 535865
Facebook: GWBurton

Games Workshop Bury
16 Crompton Street
Bury, BL9 0AD
Tel: 0161 7976540
Facebook: GWBury

Warhammer Bury St Edmunds
100 Risbygate Street
Bury St Edmunds
IP33 3AA
Tel: 01284 750745
Facebook:
WarhammerBuryStEdmunds

Warhammer Cambridge
54 Regent Street
Cambridge, CB2 1DP
Tel: 01223 313350
Facebook:
WarhammerCambridge

Warhammer Canterbury
Unit 5, Iron Bar Lane
Canterbury, CT1 2HN
Tel: 01227 452880
Facebook:
WarhammerCanterbury

Warhammer Cardiff
31 High Street, Cardiff
Glamorgan, CF10 1PU
Tel: 02920 644917
Facebook: WarhammerCardiff

Games Workshop Carlisle
Unit 2, Earls Lane
Carlisle, CA1 1DP
Tel: 01228 598216
Facebook: GWCarlisle

Games Workshop Carmarthen
19 Bridge Street
Carmarthen, SA31 3JS
Tel: 01267 231209
Facebook: GWCarmarthen

Warhammer Chatham
14 Military Road
Chatham, ME4 4JA
Tel: 01634 817287
Facebook: WarhammerChatham

Games Workshop Chelmsford
Unit 4C, Phase 2
The Meadows Centre
Chelmsford, CM2 6FD
Tel: 01245 490048
Facebook: GWChelmsford

Games Workshop Cheltenham
16 Pittville Street
Cheltenham, GL52 2LJ
Tel: 01242 228419
Facebook: GWCheltenham

Games Workshop Chester
57 Watergate Street
Chester, CH1 2LB
Tel: 01244 311 967
Facebook: GWChester

Games Workshop Chesterfield
21 Knifesmithgate
Chesterfield, S40 1RL
Tel: 01246 271118
Facebook: GWChesterfield

Warhammer Chiswick
6 Chiswick High Road
Chiswick, London, W4 1TH
Tel: 020 8994 5978
Facebook: WarhammerChiswick

Games Workshop Colchester
2 Short Wyre Street
Colchester, CO1 1LN
Tel: 01206 767279
Facebook: GWColchester

Games Workshop Coventry
Unit 39, Upper Level
Cathedral Lanes
Shopping Centre
Coventry, CV1 1LL
Tel: 02476 227311
Facebook: GWCoventry

Warhammer Crawley
11 Broadway
Crawley, RH10 1DX
Tel: 01293 552072
Facebook: WarhammerCrawley

Games Workshop Crewe
8 Market Street
Crewe, CW1 2EG
Tel: 01270 216903
Facebook: GWCrewe

Games Workshop Cribbs Causeway
Unit 129, Upper Level
The Mall At Cribbs Causeway
Bristol, BS34 5UP
Tel: 0117 9592520
Facebook: GWCribbsCauseway

Games Workshop Croydon
Unit 2, Norfolk House
Wellesley Road, CR0 1LH
Tel: 0208 680 4600
Facebook: GWCroydon

Games Workshop Cwmbran
30 The Parade, Cwmbran
Gwent, NP44 1PT
Tel: 01633 874070
Facebook: GWCwmbran

Games Workshop Darlington
78 Skinnergate
Darlington, DL3 7LX
Tel: 01325 382463
Facebook: GWDarlington

Games Workshop Derby
42 Sadler Gate
Derby, DE1 3NR
Tel: 01332 371657
Facebook: GWDerby

Games Workshop Doncaster
26 High Street
Doncaster, DN1 1DW
Tel: 01302 320535
Facebook: GWDoncaster

Games Workshop Dudley
Unit 36, Merry Hill Centre
Brierley Hill, Dudley, DY5 1SP
Tel: 01384 481818
Facebook: GWDudley

Games Workshop Dundee
110 Commercial Street
Dundee, DD1 2AJ
Tel: 01382 202382
Facebook: GWDundee

Games Workshop Durham
64 North Road
Durham, DH1 4SQ
Tel: 01913 741062
Facebook: GWDurham

Games Workshop Eastbourne
33 Cornfield Road
Eastbourne, BN21 4QG
Tel: 01323 641423
Facebook: GWEastbourne

Warhammer East Kilbride
6 Righead Gate
East Kilbride, G74 1LS
Tel: 01355 236782
Facebook:
WarhammerEastKilbride

Warhammer Edinburgh
136 High Street
Edinburgh, EH1 1QS
Tel: 01312 206540
Facebook: WarhammerEdinburgh

Games Workshop Enfield
65 Windmill Hill
Enfield, EN2 7AF
Tel: 0208 3644825
Facebook:
GamesWorkshopEnfield

Games Workshop Epsom
8 High Street
Epsom, KT19 8AD
Tel: 01372 751881
Facebook: GWEpsom

Games Workshop Exeter
31a Sidwell Street
Exeter, EX4 6NN
Tel: 01392 490305
Facebook: GWExeter

Warhammer Falkirk
12 Cow Wynd
Falkirk, FK1 1PL
Tel: 01324 624553
Facebook: WarhammerFalkirk

Warhammer Glasgow
81 Union Street
Glasgow, G1 3TA
Tel: 01412 211673
Facebook: WarhammerGlasgow

Games Workshop Gloucester
35 Clarence Street
Gloucester, GL1 1EA
Tel: 01452 505033
Facebook: GWGloucester

Games Workshop Grimsby
9 West St Mary's Gate
Grimsby, DN31 1LB
Tel: 01472 347757
Facebook: GWGrimsby

Games Workshop Guildford
Unit 1, 9/12 Tunsgate
Guildford, GU1 3QT
Tel: 01483 451793
Facebook: GWGuildford

Games Workshop Harrogate
53 Station Parade
Harrogate, HG1 1TT
Tel: 01423 564310
Facebook: GWHarrogate

Games Workshop Hemel Hempstead
117 Marlowes
Hemel Hempstead, HP1 1BB
Tel: 01442 249752
Facebook: GWHemelHempstead

Games Workshop Hereford
40 Eign Gate
Hereford, HR4 0AB
Tel: 01432 355 040
Facebook: GWHereford

Games Workshop High Wycombe
No 55 Eden Walk Gallery, Eden
High Wycombe, HP11 2HT
Tel: 01494 531494
Facebook: GWHighWycombe

Warhammer Huddersfield
9 Market Street
Huddersfield, HD1 2EH
Tel: 01484 430802
Facebook:Warhammer
Huddersfield

Games Workshop Hull
30 Paragon Street
Hull, HU1 3ND
Tel: 01482 589576
Facebook: GWHull

Games Workshop Inverness
1c Strothers Lane
Inverness, IV1 1LR
Tel: 01463 716676
Facebook: GWInverness

Games Workshop Ipswich
63 Westgate Street
Ipswich, IP1 3DZ
Tel: 01473 210 031
Facebook: GWIpswich

Warhammer Isle of Wight
35 St James Street, Newport
Isle of Wight, PO30 1LG
Tel: 01983 522 191
Facebook:
WarhammerIsleofWight

Games Workshop Kendal
Units 4 & 5 Blackhall Yard
Kendal, LA9 4LU
Tel: 01539 722211
Facebook: GWKendal

Games Workshop Kettering
4 Lower Street
Kettering, NN16 8DH
Tel: 01536 411114
Facebook: GWKettering

Games Workshop Kings Lynn
23 Norfolk Street, King's Lynn
Norfolk, PE30 1AN
Tel: 01553 777920
Facebook: GWKingsLynn

Warhammer Kingston
33 Fife Road
Kingston, KT1 1SF
Tel: 0208 5495224
Facebook: WarhammerKingston

Games Workshop Leamington Spa
32 Regent Street
Leamington Spa, CV32 5EG
Tel: 01926 435771
Facebook: GWLeamingtonSpa

Games Workshop Leeds
155 Briggate
Leeds, LS1 6LY
Tel: 0113 2420834
Facebook: GWLeeds

Warhammer Leicester
Unit 2, 16/20 Silver Street
Leicester, LE1 5ET
Tel: 0116 2530510
Facebook: WarhammerLeicester

Warhammer Lincoln
Unit SUA, Waterside Centre
Lincoln, LN2 1DH
Tel: 01522 548027
Facebook: WarhammerLincoln

Games Workshop Liverpool
13b Central Shopping Centre
Ranelagh Street
Liverpool, L1 1QE
Tel: 0151 7030963
Facebook: GWLiverpool

Games Workshop Loughborough
22 Biggin Street
Loughborough, LE11 1UA
Tel: 01509 238107
Facebook: GWLoughborough

Games Workshop Macclesfield
31 Church Street
Macclesfield, SK11 6LB
Tel: 01625 619020
Facebook: GWMacclesfield

Games Workshop Maidenhead
1 Kingsway Chambers
King Street
Maidenhead, SL6 1EE
Tel: 01628 631747
Facebook: GWMaidenhead

Games Workshop Maidstone
7a Pudding Lane
Maidstone, ME14 1PA
Tel: 01622 677435
Facebook: GWMaidstone

Games Workshop Manchester
Unit R35, Marsden Way South
Arndale Centre
Manchester, M4 3AT
Tel: 0161 8346871
Facebook: GWManchester

Games Workshop Metro Centre
23 The Boulevard
Metrocentre
Gateshead, NE11 9YG
Tel: 0191 4610950
Facebook: GWMetroCentre

Games Workshop Middlesbrough
Unit 33, 39 Dundas Street
Middlesbrough, TS1 1HR
Tel: 01642 254091
Facebook: GWMiddlesbrough

Games Workshop Milton Keynes
Unit 2, 502 Silbury Boulevard
Milton Keynes, MK9 2AD
Tel: 01908 690477
Facebook: GWMiltonKeynes

Games Workshop Muswell Hill
117 Alexandra Park Road
Muswell Hill, London, N10 2DP
Tel: 0208 8839901
Facebook: GWMuswellHill

Warhammer Newbury
114 Bartholomew Street
Newbury, RG14 5DT
Tel: 0163 540348
Facebook: WarhammerNewbury

Warhammer Newcastle
8 Hood Street
Newcastle, NE1 6JQ
Tel: 0191 2322418.
Facebook:
WarhammerNewcastle

Games Workshop Northampton
28 St. Giles Street,
Northampton, NN1 1JA
Tel: 01604 636687
Facebook: GWNorthampton

Games Workshop Norwich
12/14 Exchange Street
Norwich, NR2 1AT
Tel: 01603 767656
Facebook: GWNorwich

Games Workshop Nottingham
34A Friar Lane
Nottingham, NG1 6DQ
Tel: 0115 9480651
Facebook: GWNottingham

Games Workshop Nuneaton
3 Bridge Street
Nuneaton, CV11 4DZ
Tel: 02476 325754
Facebook: GWNuneaton

Games Workshop Oxford
1A Bush House
New Inn Hall Street
Oxford, OX1 2DH
Tel: 01865 242182
Facebook: GWOxford

Warhammer Perth
62 Scott Street
Perth, PH2 8JW
Tel: 01738 623188
Facebook: WarhammerPerthUK

Games Workshop Peterborough
3 Wentworth Street
Peterborough, PE1 1DH
Tel: 01733 890052
Facebook: GWPeterborough

Games Workshop Plymouth
84 Cornwall Street
Plymouth, PL1 1LR
Tel: 01752 254121
Facebook: GWPlymouth

Games Workshop Poole
Unit 12, Towngate Centre
High Street, Poole, BH15 1ER
Tel: 01202 685634
Facebook: GWPoole

Games Workshop Portsmouth
34 Arundel Street
Portsmouth, PO1 1NL
Tel: 02392 876266
Facebook: GWPortsmouth

Games Workshop Preston
15 Miller Arcade
Preston, PR1 2QY
Tel: 01772 821855
Facebook:
GamesWorkshopPreston

Games Workshop Putney
195 Upper Richmond Road
Putney, SW15 6SG
Tel: 020 8780 3202
Facebook: GWPutney

Games Workshop Reading
29 Oxford Road
Reading, RG1 7QA
Tel: 0118 9598693
Facebook: GWReading

Games Workshop Romford
12 Quadrant Arcade
Romford, RM1 3ED
Tel: 01708 742140
Facebook: GWRomford

Games Workshop Rotherham
17 Old Town Hall
Rotherham, S60 1QX
Tel: 01709 374520
Facebook: GWRotherham

Games Workshop Salisbury
1B Winchester Street
Salisbury, SP1 1HB
Tel: 01722 330955
Facebook: GWSalisbury

Warhammer Scarborough
9 St. Thomas Street
Scarborough, YO11 1ER
Tel: 01723 368 379
Facebook:
WarhammerScarborough

Games Workshop Sheffield
16 Fitzwilliam Gate
Sheffield, S1 4JH
Tel: 0114 2750114
Facebook: GWSheffield

Games Workshop Shrewsbury
6 Market Street
Shrewsbury, SY1 1LE
Tel: 01743 362007
Facebook: GWShrewsbury

Games Workshop Solihull
690 Warwick Road
Solihull, B91 3DX
Tel: 0121 7057997
Facebook: GWSolihull

Warhammer Southampton
23 East Street
Southampton, SO14 3HG
Tel: 02380 331962
Facebook:
WarhammerSouthampton

Games Workshop Southend
Unit G3, Victoria Centre,
Southend, SS1 2NG
Tel: 01702 461251
Facebook: GWSouthend

Games Workshop Southport
Unit 2, The Edge
7 Hoghton Street
Southport, PR9 0TE
Tel: 01704 501255
Facebook: GWSouthport

Games Workshop South Shields
17 Denmark Centre
South Shields, NE33 2LR
Tel: 01914 276798
Facebook: GWSouthShields

Games Workshop St Albans
18 Heritage Close
Off High Street
St Albans, AL3 4EB
Tel: 01727 861193
Facebook: GWStAlbans

Games Workshop Staines
8 Clarence Street
Staines, TW18 4SP
Tel: 01784 460675
Facebook: GWStaines

Games Workshop Stevenage
5 Queensway
Stevenage, SG1 1DA
Tel: 01438 355044
Facebook: GWStevenage

Games Workshop Stirling
45 Barnton Street
Stirling, FK8 1HF
Tel: 01786 459009
Facebook: GWStirling

Games Workshop Stoke
27 Stafford Street, Hanley
Stoke-on-Trent, ST1 1JU
Tel: 01782 205287
Facebook: GWStoke

Games Workshop Stockport
32 Mersey Square
Stockport, SK1 1RA
Tel: 0161 4741443
Facebook: GWStockport

Games Workshop Stratford
Unit 1, 27 Windsor Street
Stratford-upon-Avon, CV37 6NL
Tel: 01789 297262
Facebook: GWStratford

Games Workshop Sunderland
253B High Street West
Sunderland, SR1 3DH
Tel: 0191 5100434
Facebook: GWSunderland

Games Workshop Sutton
Unit 26, Times Square Shopping
Centre, Sutton, SM1 1LF
Tel: 0208 7709454
Facebook:
GamesWorkshopSutton

Games Workshop Sutton Coldfield
36 Birmingham Road
Sutton Coldfield, B72 1QQ
Tel: 0121 3543174
Facebook: GWSuttonColdfield

Games Workshop Swansea
53 Kingsway
Swansea, SA1 5HF
Tel: 01792 463969
Facebook: GWSwansea

Warhammer Swindon
22 The Plaza, The Brunel
Swindon, SN1 1LF
Tel: 01793 436036
Facebook: WarhammerSwindon

Games Workshop Taunton
Unit 9
County Walk Shopping Centre,
East Street, Taunton, TA1 3TZ
Tel: 01823 279205
Facebook: GWTaunton

Warhammer Tottenham Court Road
243 Tottenham Court Road
London, W1T 7QS
Tel: 0207 323 6408
Facebook:Warhammer
TottenhamCourtRoad

Games Workshop Truro
Unit 1 Bridge House
New Bridge Street
Truro, TR1 2AA
Tel: 01872 320047
Facebook: GWTruro

Games Workshop Tunbridge Wells
36 Grosvenor Road
Tunbridge Wells
Kent, TN1 2AP
Tel: 01892 525783
Facebook: GWTunbridgeWells

Games Workshop Twickenham
16 Church Street, Twickenham
Middlesex, TW1 3NJ
Tel: 0208 891 3936
Facebook: GWTwickenham

Games Workshop Uxbridge
231 High Street
Uxbridge, UB8 1LD
Tel: 01895 252 800
Facebook: GWUxbridge

Warhammer Wakefield
96 Kirkgate, The Ridings Centre
Wakefield, WF1 1TB
Tel: 01924 369431
Facebook: WarhammerWakefield

Games Workshop Walsall
Unit 26, Old Square Shopping
Centre, Walsall, WS1 1QF
Tel: 01922 725207
Facebook: GWWalsall

Warhammer World
Warhammer World
Willow Road, Lenton
Nottingham, NG7 2WS
Tel: 0115 9004151
Facebook: GWWarhammerWorld

Games Workshop Warrington
33 Sankey Street
Warrington, WA1 1XG
Tel: 01925 651984
Facebook: GWWarrington

Games Workshop Watford
Unit Q, 1A Queen Street
Harlequin Centre
Watford, WD17 2LH
Tel: 01923 245388
Facebook: GWWatford

Games Workshop Wigan
12 Crompton Street
Wigan, WN1 1YP
Tel: 01942 829121
Facebook: GWWigan

Games Workshop Winchester
35 Jewry Street
Winchester, SO23 8RY
Tel: 01962 860199
Facebook: GWWinchester

Games Workshop Windsor
Unit 3, 6 George V Place
Thames Avenue
Windsor, SL4 1QP
Tel: 01753 861087
Facebook: GWWindsor

Games Workshop Woking
Unit 3, Cleary Court
169 Church Street East
Woking, GU21 6HJ
Tel: 01483 771675
Facebook: GWWoking

Games Workshop Wolverhampton
9 King Street
Wolverhampton, WV1 1ST
Tel: 01902 310466
Facebook: GWWolverhampton

Games Workshop Worcester
10A College Street
Worcester, WR1 2LU
Tel: 01905 616707
Facebook: GWWorcester

Games Workshop Worthing
2 Bath Place
Worthing, BN11 3BA
Tel: 01903 213930
Facebook: GWWorthing

Games Workshop York
13a Lendal, York, YO1 8AQ
Tel: 01904 628014
Facebook:
GamesWorkshopYork

AUSTRALIA

Games Workshop Adelaide
Shop 25 Citi Centre Arcade
145 Rundle Mall
Adelaide, SA, 5000
Tel: (08) 8232 7611
Facebook: GWAdelaide

Games Workshop Albury
2/462 Dean Street
Albury, NSW, 2640
Tel: (02) 6023 1247
Facebook: GWAlbury

Games Workshop Ascot Vale
99 Union Rd
Ascot Vale, VIC, 3032
Tel: (03) 9370 9882
Facebook: GWAscotVale

Games Workshop Belconnen
Unit 5, 62 Weedon Close
Beconnen, NSW, 2617
Tel: (02) 6251 1996
Facebook: GWBelconnen

Warhammer Bendigo
40 Mitchell Street
Bendigo, VIC, 3550
Tel: (03) 5442 6191
Facebook: WarhammerBendigo

Games Workshop Blacktown
Shop 1/15 Flushcombe Rd
Blacktown, NSW, 2148
Tel: (02) 9676 5371
Facebook: GWBlacktown

Games Workshop Bondi
91 Bronte Road
Bondi Junction, NSW, 2022
Tel: (02) 9387 3347
Facebook: GWBondi

Games Workshop Brisbane
Shop 6, 420 Queen Street
Brisbane, QLD, 4000
Tel: (07) 3831 9272
Facebook: GWBrisbane

Games Workshop Broadbeach
Unit 3
2717 Gold Coast Highway
Broadbeach, QLD, 4218
Tel: (07) 5538 9992
Facebook: GWBroadbeach

Games Workshop Cairns
Shop 5 Oceana Walk
55 Lake Street
Cairns, QLD, 4870
Tel: (07) 4041 2359
Facebook:
GamesWorkshopCairns

Games Workshop Campbelltown
Shop 5, 138 Queen Street
Campbelltown, NSW, 2560
Tel: (02) 4625 6774
Facebook: GWCampbelltown

Warhammer Capalaba
Shop 6, 20 Redland Bay Road
Capalaba, QLD, 4157
Facebook: WarhammerCapalaba

Games Workshop Castle Mall
Shop 226 Castle Mall
4-16 Terminus Street
Castle Hill, NSW, 2154
Tel: (02) 9894 8284
Facebook: GWCastleMall

Games Workshop Casuarina
5B, 289 Trower Road
Casuarina, NT, 0810
Tel: (08) 8927 5116
Facebook: GWCasuarina

Games Workshop Chatswood
Shop 2, 282 Victoria Avenue
Chatswood, NSW, 2067
Tel: (02) 9415 3968
Facebook: GWChatswood

Games Workshop Cheltenham
292B Charman Road
Cheltenham, VIC, 3192
Facebook: GWCheltenhamVIC

Games Workshop Chermside
Shop 230
Westfield Shoppingtown
Cnr Gympie & Hamilton Roads
Chermside, QLD, 4032
Tel: (07) 3350 5896
Facebook: GWChermside

Games Workshop Fremantle
17 Point Street
Fremantle, WA, 6160
Tel: (08) 9336 7392
Facebook: GWFremantle

Games Workshop Geelong
167 Ryrie Street
Geelong, VIC, 3220
Tel: (03) 5221 7116
Facebook: GWGeelong

Games Workshop Hobart
125 Elizabeth Street
Hobart, TAS, 7000
Tel: (03) 6231 8471
Facebook: GWHobart

Games Workshop Hurstville
4 Cross Street
Hurstville, NSW, 2220
Tel: (02) 9585 8908
Facebook:
GamesWorkshopHurstville

Games Workshop Joondalup
Shop 5
80 Grand Boulevard
Joondalup, WA, 6027
Tel: (08) 9300 9773
Facebook: GWJoondalup

Games Workshop Launceston
81a George St
Launceston, TAS, 7250
Tel: (03) 6331 4054
Facebook: GWLaunceston

Games Workshop Liverpool
Shop 3, 170 George Street
Liverpool, NSW, 2170
Tel: (02) 9734 9030
Facebook: GWLiverpoolNSW

Games Workshop Maroochydore
Shop 7, 2 Ocean Street
Maroochydore, QLD, 4558
Tel: (07) 5443 2882
Facebook: GWMaroochydore

Games Workshop Melbourne
Shop E9 Southern Cross Lane
Little Collins Street
Melbourne, VIC, 3000
Tel: (03) 9654 7086
Facebook: GWMelbourne

Games Workshop Miranda
Shop 1 589-591 Kingsway
Miranda, NSW, 2228
Tel: (02) 9526 1966
Facebook: GWMiranda

Games Workshop Modbury
Shop 23.1 Modbury Triangle
Shopping Centre
954 North East Road
Modbury, SA, 5092
Tel: (08) 8265 4731
Facebook: GWModbury

Games Workshop Morley
Shop 2.138 Centro Galleria
Old Collier Road
Morley, WA, 6062
Tel: (08) 9375 6294
Facebook:
GamesWorkshopMorley

Games Workshop Mt. Gravatt
Office 9
Palmdale Shopping Centre
2120 Logan Road
Mt. Gravatt, QLD, 4122
Tel: (07) 3343 1864
Facebook: GWMtGravatt

Games Workshop Newcastle
197 Hunter Street
Newcastle, NSW, 2300
Tel: (02) 4926 2311
Facebook: GWNewcastleNSW

Games Workshop Oakleigh
8 Atherton Road
Oakleigh, VIC, 3166
Tel: (03) 9569 5592
Facebook: GWOakleigh

Games Workshop Parramatta
77 Phillip Street
Parramatta, NSW, 2150
Tel: (02) 9891 4543
Facebook: GWParramatta2

Warhammer Penrith
Shop 2, 495 High Street
Penrith, NSW, 2750
Facebook: WarhammerPenrith

Games Workshop Perth
Shop M18a Carillon City
Murray St
Perth, WA, 6000
Tel: (08) 9322 3895
Facebook: GWPerth

Games Workshop Preston
519 High Street
Preston, VIC, 3072
Tel: (03) 9478 0540
Facebook: GWPrestonVIC

Games Workshop Ringwood
Shop 14, 86 Maroondah Hwy
Ringwood, VIC, 3134
Tel: (03) 9870 2239
Facebook: GWRingwood

Warhammer Sydney
222 Clarence Street
Sydney, NSW, 2000
Tel: (02) 9267 6020
Facebook: WarhammerSydney

Games Workshop Townsville
Shop D Ground Floor
Northtown
280 Flinders Street
Townsville, QLD, 4810
Tel: (07) 4724 2324
Facebook:
GamesWorkshopTownsville

Games Workshop Warradale
Shop 1
241 Diagonal Road
Warradale, SA, 5046
Tel: (08) 8298 1620
Facebook: GWWarradale

Games Workshop Woden
Shop LG68C Westfield
Shoppingtown, Keltie Street
Woden, ACT, 2606
Tel: (02) 6232 5231
Facebook: GWWoden

Games Workshop Wollongong
Shop 2 (Globe Lane)
201 Crown Street
Wollongong, NSW, 2500
Tel: (02) 4225 8064
Facebook: GWWollongong

AUSTRIA

Games Workshop Innsbruck
Blasius-Hueber-Straße 16
6020 Innsbruck
Tel: (0512) 283059
Facebook: GWInnsbruck

Games Workshop Klagenfurt
8-Mai-Str. 15
Klagenfurt, 9020
Tel: (0463) 503041
Facebook: GWKlagenfurt

Warhammer Linz
Auerspergstr. 11
4020 Linz
Tel: 06929 957 1934
Facebook: WarhammerLinz

Games Workshop Wien 1
LaStafa, Mariahilferstraße 95
Wien, 1060
Tel: (01) 5223178
Facebook: GWWien1

Games Workshop Wien 2
Gasometer-City, Turm A-A30
Guglgasse 8
Wien, 1110
Tel: (01) 7431038
Facebook: GWWien2

BELGIUM

Games Workshop Antwerpen
Vleminckstraat 10
Antwerpen 2000
Tel: 03 485 86 27
Facebook: GWAntwerpen

Games Workshop Bruxelles
10 rue du Lombard
B1000 Bruxelles
Tel: 02 223 06 61
Facebook: GWBruxelles

Games Workshop Gent
St. Niklaasstraat 17a/19
Gent 9000
Tel: 09 223 91 20
Facebook: GamesWorkshopGent

Games Workshop Liège
27 rue de la Régence
B4000 Liege
Tel: 04 250 06 99
Facebook: GWLiege

Games Workshop Namur
34 rue de Fer,
B5000 Namur
Tel: 08 165 98 65
Facebook: GWNamur

CANADA

Games Workshop Appleby Village
491 Appleby Line, Unit #9
Burlington, ON, L7L 2Y1
Tel: 905-634-4584
Facebook: GWApplebyVillage

Games Workshop Chinook Centre
6455 Macleod Trail SW
Unit 0191
Calgary, AB, T2H 0K9
Tel: 403-319-0064
Facebook: GWChinook

Games Workshop Coliseum
3098 Carling Ave, Unit #7B
Ottawa, ON, K2B 7K2
Tel: 613-656-9790
Facebook: GWColiseum

Games Workshop Durham Centre
135 Harwood Avenue N
Unit B204, Ajax, ON, L1Z 1E9
Tel: 289-372-3042
Facebook: GWDurhamCentre

Warhammer Fairway Road
500 Fairway Road South, Unit 9
Kitchener, ON, N2C 1X3
Facebook:
WarhammerFairwayRoad

Games Workshop Halifax Shopping Centre
6950 Mumford Road, Unit 304
Halifax, NS, B3L 4W1
Tel: 902-442-0297
Facebook: GWHalifax

Games Workshop Heartland Towne Centre
5955 Latimer Drive, Unit #2
Mississauga, ON, L5V 0B7
Tel: (905) 858-2232
Facebook:
GWHeartlandTowneCentre

Games Workshop Highgate Village
7155 Kingsway, Suite 201
Burnaby, BC, V5E 2V1
Tel: 604-629-1064
Facebook: GWHighgateVillage

Games Workshop Kingsway Garden Mall
109 Princess Elizabeth Avenue
Unit 738
Edmonton, AB, T5G 3A6
Tel: 780-474-7166
Facebook: GWKingsway

Games Workshop Langstaff Square
8401 Weston Rd, Unit 5
Vaughan, ON, L4L 1A6
Tel: 905-850-0935
Facebook: GWLangstaffSquare

Games Workshop Montreal-EC
705 Ste-Catherine Ouest
Unit 4121
Montreal, QC, H3B 4G5
Tel: 514-844-3622
Facebook: GWMontrealEC

Games Workshop Victoria
625 Johnson Street
Victoria, BC, V8W 1M5
Tel: 250-361-1499
Facebook: GWVictoria

Games Workshop West Edmonton Mall
8882 170th Street, Unit 1788
Edmonton, AB, T5T 4J2
Tel: 780-486-3332
Facebook: GWWestEdmonton

Games Workshop White Oaks Mall
1105 Wellington Road
Unit 411
London, ON, N6E 1V4
Tel: 519-668-3713
Facebook: GWWhiteOaksMall

Games Workshop Winnipeg
200 Meadowood Drive
Unit 14
Winnipeg, MB, R2M 5G3
Tel: 204-254-4864
Facebook: GWWinnipeg

Games Workshop Yonge and Lawrence
3251 Yonge Street
Toronto, ON, M4N 2L5
Tel: 647-428-7122
Facebook:
GWYongeAndLawrence

CHINA

Warhammer Changning
722-2 Xinhua Road
Changning District
Shanghai, 200051
上海市长宁区
新华路722-2号
靠近延安西路
邮编: 200051

Games Workshop Huangpu
153-155 Xujiahui Road
Huangpu District
Shanghai, 200021
上海市黄浦区
徐家汇路153-155号
靠近蒙自路
邮编: 200021

Warhammer Parkside Plaza
Room L3-34a, 196 Daduhe Road
Putuo District
Shanghai, 200062
上海市普陀区
大渡河路196号L3-34a室
邮编: 200062

Games Workshop Pudong
Unit KJ-025, MS City
Science and Technology
Museum Subway Station
Line 2 (near Exit 6)
1170 Jingxiu Road
Pudong District
Shanghai, 200120
上海市浦东新区
锦绣路1170号
2号线科技馆地铁站
KJ-025 商铺（近6号口）
邮编: 200120

Warhammer Wanda Baoshan
Room 265, No 3, Alley 1000
128 Jinian Road
Baoshan District
Shanghai, 200435
上海市宝山区
一二八纪念路1000弄
3号265室
邮编: 200435

DENMARK 🇩🇰

Warhammer København
Skindergade 44
1159 Kobenhavn
Tel: 33 12 22 17
Facebook:
WarhammerKobenhavn

FINLAND 🇫🇮

Warhammer Helsinki
Graniittitalo Building,
Jaakonkatu 3, 00100, Helsinki
Tel: 09 7515 4525
Facebook: WarhammerHelsinki

FRANCE 🇫🇷

**Games Workshop
Aix en Provence**
33 rue de la Couronne
13100 Aix en Provence
Tel : 0 442 268 366
Facebook : GWAix

Games Workshop Amiens
2 rue des Lombards
80000 Amiens
Tel : 0 322 910 195
Facebook : GWAmiens

Games Workshop Avignon
6 rue Portail Mathéron
84000 Avignon
Tel : 0 490 840 007
Facebook : GWAvignon

**Games Workshop
Bordeaux**
63 rue des Ayres
33000 Bordeaux
Tel : 0 556 445 056
Facebook : GWBordeaux

**Games Workshop
Boulogne-Billancourt**
40 avenue du Général Leclerc
92100 Boulogne Billancourt
Tel : 0 141 039 055
Facebook:
GWBoulogneBillancourt

Games Workshop Caen
22 bis rue Froide
14000 Caen
Tel : 0 231 503 097
Facebook : GWCaen

**Games Workshop Clermont-
Ferrand**
38 avenue des États-Unis
63001 Clermont-Ferrand
Tel : 0 473 192 076
Facebook : GWClermontFerrand

Games Workshop Dijon
48 rue Berbisey
21000 Dijon
Tel : 0 380 498 766
Facebook : GWDijon

Games Workshop Grenoble
54 cours Berriat
38000 Grenoble
Tel : 0 476 864 030
Facebook : GWGrenoble

Games Workshop Le Havre
44 rue du Maréchal Gallieni
76600 Le Havre
Tel : 0 235 415 150
Facebook : GWLehavre

Games Workshop Lille
78 rue Nationale
59800 Lille
Tel : 0 320 316 989
Facebook : GWLille

**Games Workshop
Limoges**
3 rue Othon Peconnet
87000 Limoges
Tel : 0 555 103 841
Facebook : GWLimoges

Games Workshop Lyon 1
10 rue Joseph Serlin
69001 Lyon
Tel : 0 478 299 712
Facebook : GamesWorkshopLyon

Games Workshop Lyon 2
56 boulevard des Brotteaux
69006 Lyon
Tel : 0 478 262 877
Facebook: GWLyon2

Games Workshop Marseille
8 rue Armeny
13006 Marseille
Tel : 0 491 570 145
Facebook: GWMarseille

Games Workshop Metz
52 En Fournirue
57000 Metz
Tel : 0 387 746 620
Facebook: GWMetz

Games Workshop Montpellier
2 rue Draperie Saint-Firmin
34000 Montpellier
Tel : 0 467 586 890
Facebook: GWMontpellier

Games Workshop Mulhouse
5, rue des Tanneurs
68100 Mulhouse
Tel : 0 389 662 621
Facebook: GWMulhouse

Games Workshop Nancy
10 rue Saint-Dizier
54000 Nancy
Tel : 0 383 306 256
Facebook: GWNancy

Games Workshop Nantes
9 rue du Moulin
44000 Nantes
Tel : 0 240 891 045
Facebook: GWNantes

Games Workshop Nice
19 Rue de l'hôtel des postes
06000 Nice
Tel : 0 493 925 222
Facebook: GWNice

Games Workshop Nîmes
5 rue des Fourbisseurs
30000 Nîmes
Tel : 0 466 213 709
Facebook: GWNimes

Games Workshop Orléans
12 rue des Carmes
45000 Orléans
Tel : 0 238 628 012
Facebook: GWOrleans

Games Workshop Paris 06
10 rue Hautefeuille
75006 Paris
Tel : 0 146 332 001
Facebook: GWParis06

Warhammer Paris 08
7 rue Intérieure
75008 Paris
Tel : 0 144 700 060
Facebook : WarhammerParis08

Games Workshop Paris 09
125 rue du Faubourg
Poissonnière
75009 Paris
Tel : 09 64 42 02 42
Facebook: GWParis09

Games Workshop Paris 12
38 avenue Daumesnil
75012 Paris
Tel : 0 153 447 182
Facebook: GWParis12

Games Workshop Paris 14
13 rue Poirier de Narçay
75014 Paris
Tel : 0 145 457 203
Facebook : GWParis14

Games Workshop Paris 15
161 rue Lecourbe
75015 Paris
Tel : 0 148 562 398
Facebook: GWParis15

Games Workshop Pau
6 rue Bordenave d'Abère
64000 Pau
Tel : 0 559 052 285
Facebook : GWPau

Warhammer Perpignan
13 Rue de l'Argenterie,
66000 Perpignan
Tel : 0 468 342 343
Facebook :
WarhammerPerpignan

Games Workshop Reims
10 avenue Jean Jaurès
51100, Reims
Tel : 03 26 35 57 67
Facebook: GWReims

Games Workshop Rennes
3 rue du Vau Saint-Germain
35000 Rennes
Tel : 0 299 791 180
Facebook : GWRennes

Games Workshop Rouen
23/25 rue Alsace Lorraine
76000 Rouen
Tel : 0 235 701 208
Facebook : GWRouen

Games Workshop Strasbourg
5 rue des Frères
67000 Strasbourg
Tel : 0 388 320 806
Facebook : GWStrasbourg

Games Workshop Toulouse
13 rue Temponières
31000 Toulouse
Tel : 0 561 225 257
Facebook : GWToulouse

Games Workshop Tours
19 rue Néricault-Destouches,
37000 Tours
Tel : 0 247 613 765
Facebook :
GamesWorkshopTours

Games Workshop Versailles
10 avenue du Gal de Gaulle
78000 Versailles
Tel : 0 139 209 281
Facebook : GWVersailles

GERMANY

Warhammer Aachen
Wirichsbongardstraße 39
Aachen, 52062
Tel: (0241) 99761185
Facebook: WarhammerAachen

Games Workshop Augsburg
Schaezlerstraße 2
Augsburg, 86150
Tel: (0821) 5439507
Facebook: GWAugsburg

Games Workshop Berlin 1
Europacenter, Laden 30
Berlin, 10789
Tel: (030) 88683691
Facebook: GWBerlin1

Games Workshop Berlin 2
Frankfurter Allee 96
Berlin, 10247
Tel: (030) 29049390
Facebook: GWBerlin 2

Games Workshop Bielefeld
Obernstrasse 43
Bielefeld, 33602
Tel: (0521) 7853709
Facebook: GWBielefeld

Games Workshop Bochum
City Passage, Laden 5,
Hans Böckler Str. 12-16
Bochum, 44787
Tel: (0234) 7927045
Facebook: GWBochum

Games Workshop Bonn
Kasernenstraße 8-10
Bonn, 53111
Tel: (0228) 9610901
Facebook: GWBonn

**Games Workshop
Braunschweig**
Münzstraße 10
Braunschweig, 38100
Tel: (0531) 2083123
Facebook: GWBraunschweig

Games Workshop Bremen
Am Wall 113, Bremen, 28195
Tel: (0421) 1690000
Facebook: GWBremen

Games Workshop Darmstadt
Wilhelminenpassage, Laden 2
Darmstadt, 64283
Tel: (06151) 158845
Facebook: GWDarmstadt

Games Workshop Dortmund
Hansastraße 95
Dortmund, 44137
Tel: (0231) 141001
Facebook: GWDortmund

Games Workshop Dresden
Schweriner Str. 23
Dresden, 01067
Tel: (0351) 2069715
Facebook: GWDresden

**Games Workshop
Düsseldorf (Drakenburg)**
Am Wehrhahn 32
40211 Düsseldorf
Tel: (0211) 17544090
Facebook: GWDrakenburg

Games Workshop Duisburg
Sonnenwall 39
Duisburg, 47051
Tel: (0203) 9410673
Facebook: GWDuisburg

Games Workshop Erfurt
Weitergasse 3
99084 Erfurt
Tel: 361 644 171 33
Facebook: GWErfurt

Games Workshop Essen
Kettwiger Straße 45
Essen, 45127
Tel: (0201) 2698920
Facebook: GWEssen

Games Workshop Frankfurt
Große Friedberger Str. 30
Frankfurt, 60313
Tel: (069) 26010466
Facebook: GWFrankfurt

Games Workshop Freiburg
Konvikstr. 10a/b
(Oberlindenpassage)
Freiburg, 79098
Tel: (0761) 3844527
Facebook: GWFreiburg

Games Workshop Halle
Große Ulrichstraße 35
Halle, 06108
Tel: (0345) 29989953
Facebook: GWHalle

Games Workshop Hamburg 1
Colonnaden 15
Hamburg, 20354
Tel: (040) 35713164
Facebook: GWHamburg1

Games Workshop Hamburg 2
Geschäftszentrum, Heegbarg 4
Hamburg, 22391
Tel: (040) 18989247
Facebook: GWHamburg2

Games Workshop Hannover
Lange Laube 1/1a
Hannover, 30159
Tel: (0511) 1613808
Facebook: GWHannover

Games Workshop Ingolstadt
Hallstraße 8
Ingolstadt, 85049
Tel: (0)841 13237395
Facebook: GWIngolstadt

Games Workshop Karlsruhe
Karlstraße 13
Karlsruhe, 76133
Tel: (0721) 957761108
Facebook: GWKarlsruhe

Games Workshop Kassel
Wilhemstraße 31
Kassel, 34117
Tel: (0561) 7668 7696
Facebook: GWKassel

Games Workshop Kiel
Kehdenstraße 24
Kiel, 24103
Tel: (0431) 88786947
Facebook: GWKiel

Games Workshop Darmstadt
Wilhelminenpassage, Laden 2
Darmstadt, 64283
Tel: (06151) 158845
Facebook: GWDarmstadt

Games Workshop Köln
Cäcilienstraße 42-44
Köln, 50667
Tel: (0221) 2577707
Facebook: GWKoln1

Games Workshop Krefeld
Ostwall 113
Krefeld, 47798
Tel: (02151) 7679046
Facebook: GWKrefeld

Games Workshop Leipzig
Burgplatz 2
Leipzig, 04109
Tel: (0341) 2618924
Facebook: GWLeipzig

Games Workshop Leverkusen
Wiesdorser Platz 80b
Leverkusen, 51373
Tel: (02148) 6919480
Facebook: GWLeverkusen

Games Workshop Lübeck
Königstraße 113-119
Lübeck, 23552
Tel: (0451) 9892206
Facebook: GWLuebeck

Warhammer Mainz
Große Bleiche 6,
55116 Mainz
Tel (6131) 2148450
Facebook: WarhammerMainz

Games Workshop Mannheim
D3,4 Plankengalerie
Laden 20
Mannheim, 68159
Tel: (0621) 4053390
Facebook: GWMannheim

**Games Workshop
Mönchengladbach**
Bismarckstraße 15
Mönchengladbach, 41061
Tel: (02161) 406 7745
Facebook: GWGladbach

Games Workshop Mülheim
Leineweberstraße 41-43
Mülheim, 45468
Tel: (0208) 65634018
Facebook: GWMulheim

Warhammer München
Rumfordstraße 9, Laden 3
München, 80469
Tel: (089) 22801980
Facebook:
WarhammerMuenchen1

Games Workshop Münster
Bahnhofstr. 1-11
Münster 48143
Tel: 0251 98119840
Facebook: GWMunster

Games Workshop Neuss
Oberstr. 121 (Eingang An der
Münze), Neuss, 41460
Tel: (0)2131 2096500
Facebook: GWNeuss

Games Workshop Nürnberg
Jakobstraße 26
Nürnberg, 90402
Tel: 0049 911 37855677
Facebook: GWNuernberg

Games Workshop Oberhausen
CentrO, Centroallee 18
Einheit F05
Oberhausen, 46047
Tel: (0208) 202180
Facebook: GWOberhausen

Games Workshop Oldenburg
Markt 2-3, Eingang
Pistolenstraße
Oldenburg, 26122
Tel: (0441) 20099318
Facebook: GWOldenburg

Games Workshop Paderborn
Marienstraße 5
Paderborn, 33098
Tel: (0525)15069999
Facebook: GWPaderborn

Games Workshop Pforzheim
Goethestraße 31
Pforzheim, 75173
Tel: (07231) 9385753
Facebook: GWPforzheim

Games Workshop Potsdam
Friedrich-Ebert-Straße 114a
Potsdam, 14467
Tel: (0331) 2902950
Facebook: GWPotsdam

Games Workshop Solingen
Ufergarten 33
Solingen, 42651
Tel: (0212) 22662154
Facebook: GWSolingen

Games Workshop Spandau
Breite Straße 42
Berlin, 13597
Tel: (030) 53674909
Facebook: GWSpandau

Games Workshop Stuttgart
Königstraße 49
Stuttgart, 70173
Tel: (0711) 2294860
Facebook: GWStuttgart

Games Workshop Trier
Treviris-Passage, Laden 1a
Moselstraße 6
Trier, 54290
Tel: (0651) 46372276
Facebook: GWTrier

Games Workshop Ulm
Frauenstraße 25
Ulm, 89073
Tel: (0731) 37855695
Facebook: GWUlm

Games Workshop Wiesbaden
Friedrichstraße 34-36
Wiesbaden, 65185
Tel: (0611) 4459852
Facebook: GWWiesbaden

Games Workshop Wuppertal
Morianstraße 3
Wuppertal, 42103
Tel: (0202) 5141777
Facebook: GWWuppertal

Warhammer Würzburg
Augustinerstr. 18
Würzburg, 97070
Tel: (9314) 6586800
Facebook: WarhammerWurzburg

IRELAND

Warhammer Cork
1-2 St Patrick's Quay
Cork
Tel: 00 353 2145 03232
Facebook: WarhammerCork

Games Workshop Dublin
Unit 3, Lower Liffey Street
Dublin 1
Tel: 00 353 1872 5791
Facebook: GWDublin

ITALY

Games Workshop Bologna
Piazza F.D. Roosevelt 4/B 40121
Bologna, Emilia Romagna
Tel: 051 65 69 825
Facebook: GWBologna

Games Workshop Ferrara
Via Contrari 31, 44121, Ferrara
Tel: 0532 24 30 61
Facebook: GWFerrara

Games Workshop Firenze
Borgo San Frediano 24/R 50124
Firenze, Toscana
Tel: 055 21 06 38
Facebook: GWFirenze

Games Workshop Genova
Salita S. Maria degli Angeli 4/R
16124, Genova, Liguria
Tel: 010 25 30 472
Facebook: GWGenova

Games Workshop Milano
Via Torino 68, 20123
Milano, Lombardia
Tel: 02 864 584 90
Facebook: GWMilano

Games Workshop Modena
Via F. Selmi 60, 41121
Modena, Emilia Romagna
Tel: 059 23 76 80
Facebook: GWModena

Games Workshop Monza
Via P.R. Giuliani 10, 20052
Monza, Lombardia
Tel: 039 39 02 534
Facebook: GWMonza

Games Workshop Padova
Via del Santo 67, 35123
Padova, Veneto
Tel: 049 87 51 651
Facebook: GWPadova

Games Workshop Roma
Via Etruria 3, 00183
Roma, Lazio
Tel: 06 70 17 609
Facebook: GWRoma

Games Workshop Roma 3
Via Nemorense 41/A, 00199
Roma, Lazio
Tel: 06 85 49 821
Facebook: GWRoma3

Games Workshop Torino
Via San Dalmazzo 3, 10122
Torino, Piemonte
Tel: 011 56 28 472
Facebook: GWTorino

Games Workshop Verona
Largo San Nazaro, 2, 37129
Verona
Tel: 04 58 01 36 61
Facebook: GWVerona

JAPAN

Warhammer Jinbocho
Jinbocho 1-1-1F, Kanda
Chiyoda-ku, Tokyo
Tel: 03-3296-2733
Facebook: GW.Jinbocho
ウォーハンマーストア神保町
東京都千代田区神田神保町1-1
ゲームズワークショップビル1F

Warhammer Harajuku
Bellwood Harajuku 1F-B
3-20-21, Jingu-mae
Shibuya-ku, Tokyo
Tel: 03-6804-2170
Facebook: GW.Harajuku
ウォーハンマーストア原宿
東京都渋谷区神宮前3-20-21
ベルウッド原宿1F-B

NETHERLANDS

Games Workshop Alkmaar
Laat 68, 1811EK
Tel: 072 5122880
Facebook: GWAlkmaar

Games Workshop Amersfoort
Koestraat 20, 3811 HK
Tel: 033 4654423
Facebook: GWAmersfoort

Games Workshop Amsterdam South
Van Woustraat 69-hs, 1074 AD
Tel: 020 6645771
Facebook: GWAmsterdamSouth

Games Workshop Amsterdam West
Rozengracht 99
Amsterdam, 1016 LT
Tel: 020 6232800
Facebook: GWAmsterdamWest

Games Workshop Breda
Torenstraat 21, 4811 XV
Tel: 076 5229277
Facebook: GWBreda

Games Workshop Den Haag
Schoolstraat 12B, 2511 AX
Tel: 070 3927836
Facebook: GWDenHaag

Warhammer Deventer
Golstraat 7, 7411 BN
Tel: 057 0600838
Facebook: DeventerWarhammer

Games Workshop Eindhoven
Kleine Berg 50, 5611JV
Tel: 040 2443448
Facebook: GWEindhoven

Warhammer Enschede
Korte Haaksbergerstraat 30-30a,
Enschede, 7500
Tel: 0031 534 319163
Facebook: WarhammerEnschede

Games Workshop Groningen
Grote Kromme Elleboog 1
9712 BJ
Tel: 050 3110101
Facebook: GWGroningen

Warhammer Nijmegen
Stikke Hezelstraat 3
Nijmegen, 6511JX
Tel: 0031 24 323 3474
Facebook: WarhammerNijmegen

Games Workshop Rotterdam
452 Van Oldenbarneveltplaats
3012 AP
Tel: 010 2800268
Facebook: GWRotterdam

Games Workshop Tilburg
Korvelseweg 58,
JJ te Tilburg, 5025
Tel: 013 5433735
Facebook: GWTilburg

Warhammer Utrecht
Zakkendragersteeg 7,
3511 AA Utrecht
Tel: 030 2318887
Facebook: WarhammerUtrecht

Warhammer Zwolle
Sassenstraat 15,
8011 PA, Zwolle
Tel: 0031 0384218026
Facebook: WarhammerZwolle

NEW ZEALAND

Warhammer Dunedin
326 George Street
Dunedin, 9016
Facebook: WarhammerDunedin

Games Workshop Lower Hutt
Shop 10, Queens Arcade
65-71 Queens Drive
Lower Hutt, 5045
Tel: 644 576 0588
Facebook: GWLowerHutt

Games Workshop Mt Albert
Shop 2, 945 New North Road
Mt Albert, Auckland, 1025
Tel: 649 846 3008
Facebook: GWMtAlbert

Games Workshop Wellington
Shop T5b Courtenay Central
80 Courtenay Place
Wellington, 6011
Tel: 644 382 9532
Facebook: GamesWorkshopWellington

NORWAY

Games Workshop Oslo
Mollergata 5/9, 179, Oslo
Tel: 22 33 29 90
Facebook: GWOslo

POLAND

Games Workshop Warsaw
Ul. Zlota 59, Zlota Tarasy nr 215,
00120, Warsaw
Tel: 022 222 0133
Facebook: GWWarsaw

SPAIN

Games Workshop Argüelles
C/ Andrés Mellado 10
Madrid, 28015
Tel: 91 544 22 92
Facebook: GWArguelles

Games Workshop Badalona
C/ Sant Joaquim, 40 Badalona
Barcelona, 08911
Tel: 93 464 24 00
Facebook: GWBadalona

Games Workshop Bernabeu
C/ Panamá, 2, Madrid, 28046
Tel: 91 457 83 81
Facebook: GWBernabeu

Games Workshop Bilbao
Pérez Galdós 3, Bilbao
Bizkaia, 48010
Tel: 94 444 31 08
Facebook: GWBilbao

Games Workshop Déu i Mata
C/ Déu i Mata, 96
(esquina Prat d'en Rull)
Barcelona, 08029
Tel: 93 410 15 21
Facebook: GWDeuiMata

Games Workshop Gaudí
C/ Castillejos, 333 08025
Barcelona.
Tel: 93 436 87 82
Facebook: GWGaudi

Games Workshop Girona
C/ Sant Joan Baptista de La
Salle, 39, Girona, 17004
Tel: 97 222 73 18
Facebook: GWGirona

Games Workshop Goya
Duque de Sesto, 22,
Madrid, 28009
Tel: 91 577 21 87
Facebook: GWGoya

Games Workshop Málaga
C/ Don Cristian, 16, Málaga
29007. Tel: 952 42 96 48
Facebook: GWMalaga

Games Workshop Palma
C/ Sant Joan de la Salle, 2
Palma de Mallorca, 07003
Tel: 971 75 84 79
Facebook: GWPalma

Games Workshop Pamplona
Avenida Pio XII 6
Pamplona-Iruña
Navarra, 31008
Tel: 948 25 92 74
Facebook: GWPamplona

Games Workshop Roger de Llúria
Roger de Llúria, 53 (entre Aragó
y Consell de Cent)
Barcelona, 08009
Tel: 93 272 69 76
Facebook: GWRogerdeLluria

Games Workshop Sevilla
C/ José Laguillo 12
Sevilla, 41003
Tel: 95 490 06 24
Facebook: GWSevilla

Warhammer Tres Aguas
Avenida America 7-9
Alcorcon, Madrid, 28922
Tel: 916 10 16 50
Facebook: WarhammerTresAguas

Games Workshop València
C/ Roger de Lauria 11
València, 46002
Tel: 96 351 57 27
Facebook: GWValencia

Games Workshop Valladolid
Pza Portugalete 7,
47002, Valladolid
Tel: 983 30 12 81
Facebook: GWValladolid

Games Workshop Zaragoza
C/ Francisco de Vitoria 14
(esquina León XIII)
Zaragoza, 50008
Tel: 976 21 57 42
Facebook: GWZaragoza

SWEDEN

Games Workshop Göteborg
Drottninggatan 52
41107, Göteborg
Tel: 031-133958
Facebook: GWGoteborg

Games Workshop Stockholm
Mäster Samuelsgatan 67 11121,
Stockholm
Tel: 08-21 38 40
Facebook: GWStockholm

USA

Warhammer 8th Street
55 East 8th Street
New York, NY, 10003
Tel: 212-982-6314
Facebook: Warhammer8thStreet

Games Workshop Acadia
947 Burlington Avenue
Downers Grove, IL, 60515
Tel: 630-515-1482
Facebook: GWAcadia

Warhammer Ann Arbor
Lamp Post Plaza
2366 East Stadium Blvd
Ann Arbor, MI 48104
Facebook: WarhammerAnnArbor

Games Workshop Blue Diamond Crossing
4270 Blue Diamond Rd
Suite #104
Las Vegas, NV, 89139
Tel: 702-432-3008
Facebook: GWBlueDiamond

Games Workshop Blue Ridge Crossing
4279 Sterling Ave,
Kansas City, MO, 64133
Tel: 816-313-6492
Facebook: GWBlueRidgeCrossing

Games Workshop Bowie Bunker
6820 Race Track Rd
Bowie, MD, 20715
Tel: 301-464-4651
Facebook: GWBowie

Games Workshop Brodie Oaks Shopping Center
4032 South Lamar Boulevard
Suite 600, Austin, TX, 78704
Tel: 512-383-8660
Facebook: GWBrodieOaks

Games Workshop Capella Centre II
8653 Sancus Blvd
Columbus, OH, 43240
Tel: 614-846-2270
Facebook: GWCapellaCentre

Games Workshop Central Avenue
919 S. Central Avenue, Unit A
Glendale, CA, 91204
Tel: 818-241-0068
Facebook: GWCentralAvenue

Games Workshop Chesterfield Crossing
1639 Clarkson Road
Chesterfield, MO, 63017
Tel: 636-536-6937
Facebook: GWChesterfieldCrossing

Games Workshop City Walk
227 Sandy Springs Place
Suite #108
Sandy Springs, GA, 30328
Tel: 404-256-6439
Facebook: GWCityWalk

Games Workshop Columbia Palace
8775 Centre Park Drive
Suite 9, Columbia, MD, 21045
Tel: 410-772-3988
Facebook: GWColumbiaPalace

Games Workshop Cool Springs Village
1945 Mallory Lane
Suite #155
Franklin, TN, 37067
Tel: 615-778-3280
Facebook: GWCoolSprings

Warhammer Cornerbrook Plaza
Cornerbrook Plaza
343 Gorham Road
South Portland, ME 04106
Facebook:
WarhammerCornerbrookPlaza

Games Workshop Cottman Avenue
2141 Cottman Avenue
Suite B
Philadelphia, PA, 19149
Tel: 215-722-6187
Facebook: GWCottman

Games Workshop Deer Grove
605 East Dundee Rd.,
Palatine, IL, 60074
Tel: 847-963-1434
Facebook: GWDeerGrove

Games Workshop Deerwood Village
9978-3A Old Baymeadows Road,
Jacksonville, FL, 32256
Tel: 904-565-9241
Facebook: GWDeerwoodVillage

Games Workshop Denton Towne Crossing
1931 S Loop 288, #120
Denton, TX, 76205
Tel: 940-484-5400
Facebook:
GWDentonTownCrossing

Games Workshop Eastgate Shopping Center
6721 Eastgate Boulevard
Mayfield Heights, OH, 44124
Tel: 440-646-9706
Facebook: GWEastgate

Games Workshop Eastport Plaza
4104 SE 82nd Ave, Suite 350
Portland, OR, 97266
Tel: 503-788-7643
Facebook: GWEastportPlaza

Games Workshop Entrada De Oro
7925 North Oracle Road
Oro Valley, AZ, 85704
Tel: 520-742-7320
Facebook: GWEntradaDeOro

Games Workshop Forest Park
4711 Forest Dr, Suite #20
Columbia, SC, 29206
Tel: 803-790-6582
Facebook: GWForestPark

Games Workshop Fountain Place
12557 Castlemoor Drive
Eden Prairie, MN, 55344
Tel: 952-944-4036
Facebook: GWFountainPlace

Games Workshop Freeway V
20101 44th Avenue West
Suite D, Lynnwood, WA, 98036
Tel: 425-775-0107
Facebook: GWFreewayV

Games Workshop Garden Park Plaza
4378 Northlake Blvd.
Palm Beach Gardens,
FL, 33410
Tel: 561-775-7760
Facebook: GWGardenParkPlaza

Games Workshop Geneva Commons
1052 Commons Drive
Geneva, IL, 60134
Tel: 630-232-2929
Facebook: GWGenevaCommons

Games Workshop Hampton Village
2929 S Rochester Road
Suite 112301
Rochester Hills, MI, 48307.
Tel: 248-844-2628
Facebook: GWHamptonVillage

Warhammer High Point
202 High Point Drive
Victor, NY. 14564
Tel: (585) 425-8988
Facebook: WarhammerHighPoint

Games Workshop Hill Country Plaza
4079 N Loop 1604 W, #104
San Antonio, TX, 78257
Tel: 210-764-2200
Facebook: GWHillCountryPlaza

Games Workshop Hilltop East Shopping Center
1564 Laskin Rd, Unit 172
Virginia Beach, VA, 23451
Tel: 757-962-5259
Facebook: GWHilltopEast

Games Workshop Hyde Park Plaza
3870 Paxton Avenue, Suite B
Cincinnati, OH, 45209
Tel: 513-321-1104
Facebook: GWHydeParkPlaza

Games Workshop Kent Station
417 Ramsey Way Suite 109,
Kent, WA, 98032
Tel: 253-850-6062
Facebook: GWKentStation

Games Workshop Lake Crest Village
1050 Florin Road
Sacramento, CA, 95831
Tel: 916-392-1495
Facebook: GWLakeCrestVillage

Games Workshop Lake Shore
4155 Mountain Road
Pasadena, MD, 21122
Tel: 410-255-0596
Facebook: GWLakeShore

Games Workshop Lakeview Plaza
15766 S. LaGrange Road
Orland Park, IL 60462
Tel: 708-226-9563
Facebook: GWLakeviewPlaza

Games Workshop Larwin Square
650 East 1st Street
Tustin, CA, 92780
Tel: 714-731-3304
Facebook: GWLarwinSquare

Games Workshop Layton Plaza
7497 West Layton Avenue
Greenfield, WI, 53220
Tel: 414-325-2990
Facebook: GWLaytonPlaza

Games Workshop Mallard Pointe Shopping Center
9211 N. Tryon Street, Suite #11-A, Charlotte, NC, 28262
Tel: 704-595-9420
Facebook: GWMallardPointe

Games Workshop Man O War Place
115 North Locust Hill Drive
Suite 106
Lexington, KY, 40509
Tel: 859-266-0245
Facebook: GWManOWar

Games Workshop Meadows on the Parkway
14800 Baseline Road, A111
Boulder, CO, 80303

Games Workshop Morningside Plaza
1018 East Bastanchury Road
Fullerton, CA, 92835
Tel: 714-255-9801
Facebook: GWMorningsidePlaza

Games Workshop North Heights Plaza
8272 Old Troy Pike
Huber Heights, OH, 45424
Tel: 937-237-2280
Facebook:
GWNorthernHeightsPlaza

Warhammer North Woods
1283 Bruce B. Downs Blvd,
Wesley Chapel, FL 33544
Tel: 813-973-0450
Facebook:
WarhammerNorthwoodsCenter

Games Workshop Oakbrook Plaza
1724 E. Avenida de los Arboles,
Unit D
Thousand Oaks, CA, 91360
Tel: 805-492-8800
Facebook: GWOakbrookPlaza

Games Workshop Pender Village
3903 Fair Ridge Drive, Suite D
Fairfax, VA 22033
Tel: 703-218-1881
Facebook: GWPenderVillage

Games Workshop Pinecrest Pointe
9101 Leesville Rd, Suite #119
Raleigh, NC, 27613
Tel: 919-848-2958
Facebook: GWPinecrestPointe

Games Workshop Plaza Rancho Penasquitos
9995 Carmel Mountain Road
Suite B-5
San Diego, CA, 92129
Tel: 858-484-3074
Facebook: GWPlazaPenasquitos

Games Workshop Portola Plaza
27676 Santa Margarita Parkway
Mission Viejo, CA, 92691
Tel: 949-457-1664
Facebook: GWPortolaPlaza

Games Workshop Prairie Ridge
9740 76th Street, Space 106
Pleasant Prairie, WI, 53158
Tel: 262-697-0471
Facebook: GWPrairieRidge

Games Workshop Preston Ridge
3231 Preston Road, Suite #14
Frisco, TX, 75034
Tel: 214-618-9788
Facebook: GWPrestonRidge

Games Workshop Quail Spring Village
13801 N. Penn, Suite F
Oklahoma City, OK, 73134
Tel: 405-286-0033
Facebook: GWQuailSpring

Games Workshop Red Top Plaza
1314 S Milwaukee Ave
Libertyville, IL, 60048
Tel: 847-573-1547
Facebook: GWRedTopPlaza

Games Workshop Riverbend
622 S. Carrollton Avenue
New Orleans, LA, 70118
Tel: 504-865-0151
Facebook: GWRiverbend

Games Workshop Riverchase Promenade
1717 Montgomery Hwy
Birmingham, AL, 35244
Tel: 205-403-2750
Facebook: GWRiverchase

Games Workshop Royal Oaks
11803 Westheimer Road
Suite 700, Houston, TX, 77077
Tel: 281-556-5542
Facebook: GWRoyalOak

Games Workshop Scottsdale Towne Center
15678 N Frank Lloyd Wright
Blvd, Suite C-2
Scottsdale, AZ, 85260
Tel: 480-767-2078
Facebook:
GWScottsdaleTowneCenter

Games Workshop Shoppes at Woodruff
1451 Woodruff Road
Suite L, Greenville, SC, 29607
Tel: 864-627-4179
Facebook:
GWShoppesAtWoodruff

Games Workshop Silas Creek Crossing
3290 Silas Creek Parkway
Unit 54
Winston Salem, NC, 27103
Tel: 336-765-5476
Facebook: GWSilasCreek

Games Workshop Square One Denver
1112 South Colorado Blvd
Glendale, CO, 80246
Tel: 303-759-5400
Facebook: GWSquareOneDenver

Games Workshop Stony Brook East
9150A Taylorsville Road
Louisville, KY, 40299
Tel: 502-499-9152
Facebook: GWStonyBrookEast

Games Workshop Sunrise Village
10228 156th St. East,
Suite 106
Puyallup, WA, 98374
Tel: 253-848-5670
Facebook: GWSunriseVillage

Games Workshop Tacoma Place
1909 S. 72nd Street, Suite A7,
Tacoma, WA, 98408
Tel: 253-471-5359
Facebook: GWTacomaPlace

Games Workshop The Gateway at Sawgrass
117 NW 136th Ave
Sunrise, FL, 33325
Tel: 954-846-9415
Facebook:
GWGatewayAtSawgrass

Warhammer The Summit
13979 S Virginia Street,
Suite 503, Reno, NV, 89511
Tel: 775-851-9122
Facebook:
WarhammerTheSummit

Games Workshop Tower Center
6810 Bland St. Springfield,
VA, 22150
Tel: 703-569-1781
Facebook: GWTowerCenter

Warhammer Turkey Creek
10913 Parkside Drive
Knoxville, TN. 37934
Tel: 865-675-6000
Facebook:
WarhammerTurkeyCreek

Games Workshop Union Landing
30977 Courthouse Drive
Union City, CA, 94587
Tel: 510-429-1759
Facebook: GWUnionLanding

Games Workshop Ventura Village
5722 Telephone Road, Suite
14-B, Ventura, CA, 93003
Tel: 805-339-9580
Facebook: GWVenturaVillage

Games Workshop Village Center
23730 Westheimer Pkwy,
Suite P, Katy, TX, 77494
Tel: 281-347-0400
Facebook: GWVillageCenter

Games Workshop West Hartford
7 South Main Street,
West Hartford, CT, 06107
Tel: 860-702-1138
Facebook: GWWestHartford

Warhammer Westbury Square
975 Airport Road SW, Suite 14
Huntsville, AL, 35802
Tel: 256-881-7733
Facebook:
WarhammerWestburySquare

Games Workshop Westminster Center
6735 Westminster Blvd
Suite F, Westminster,
CA 92683
Tel: 714-892-2973
Facebook: GWWestminsterCtr

Games Workshop Westwood Plaza
2808 S 123rd Ct.
Omaha, NE, 68144
Tel: 402-330-4958
Facebook: GWWestminsterCtr

Games Workshop Willow Lake East
2502 Lake Circle Dr
Indianapolis, IN, 46268
Tel: 317-228-9578
Facebook: GWWillowLake

Warhammer Winter Park
480 North Orlando Ave,
Suite 122
Winter Park, FL. 32789
Tel: 407-622-4966
Facebook:
WarhammerWinterPark

Games Workshop World of Battle
6211 East Holmes Road, Suite
101, Memphis, TN, 38141
Tel: 901-541-7700
Facebook: GWWorldOfBattle

For complete, up-to-date listings of Games Workshop Stores and Independent Stockists, go to:

Pour consulter la liste complète et à jour des magasins et détaillants Games Workshop, rendez-vous sur:

Für eine vollständige, aktuelle Liste aller Games-Workshop-Läden und unabhängigen Einzelhändler besuche:

WWW.GAMES-WORKSHOP.COM/STORE-FINDER

SUBSCRIPTIONS

SUBSCRIBE TO WARHAMMER VISIONS AND WHITE DWARF – AND GET YOUR FAVOURITE GAMES WORKSHOP MAGS DELIVERED STRAIGHT TO YOUR FRONT DOOR!

WARHAMMER VISIONS

Warhammer Visions is Games Workshop's monthly photographic showcase of the worlds of Warhammer, sporting the most amazing painted miniatures around, with features such as Army of the Month and Blanchitsu.

UK Subscribers can take out a Direct Debit to Warhammer Visions for the great price of £15 per quarter – that's three issues for the price of two! Contact UK Customer Services.

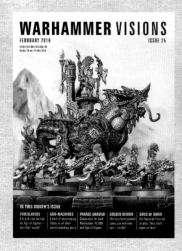

12 issues for £65 / €80 / $100usa / $110can / $120aus / $190nz / 840skr / 900nkr / 760dkr – go to games-workshop.com

WARHAMMER VISIONS IPAD EDITION SUBSCRIPTION ALSO AVAILABLE

WHITE DWARF

White Dwarf is your weekly guide to what's new and exciting from Games Workshop, featuring the latest releases, rules, painting guides, in-depth features, battle reports and much, much more – every Saturday!

6 month (26 issues) and 12 month (52 issues) subscriptions available from games-workshop.com

6 month subscription £65 / €100 / $100usa / $130can / $150aus / $190nz / 950skr / 850nkr / 750dkr

12 month subscription £120 / €190 / $190usa / $250can / $290aus / $360nz / 1800skr / 1600nkr / 1400dkr

SUBSCRIBE TO BOTH WARHAMMER VISIONS AND WHITE DWARF!

We're pleased to also offer a combined subscription to both Warhammer Visions and White Dwarf – you need never miss an issue of either magazine again!

12 months for £175 / €260 / $275usa / $350can / $390aus / $525nz / 2640skr / 2500nkr / 2160dkr – go to games-workshop.com

Customer Services contact details:

PARTING SHOT

"Bringers of Doom; Avenging Angels of Death; they are the

"Porteurs du Jugement ; Anges de la Mort; on les appelle les

"Boten des Verderbens; Engel der Rache und des Todes; die